THE TOP TEN FAMILY STRESSES

✦   ✦   ✦

1. Economics/finances/budgeting
2. Children's behavior/discipline/sibling fighting
3. Not enough couple time
4. Lack of shared responsibility in the family
5. Communicating with children
6. Not enough "me" time
7. Guilt for not getting enough done
8. Spousal relationship (communication, friendship, sex)
9. Not enough family playtime
10. Overscheduled family calendar

Read on and discover a wealth of creative tips to help *your* family triumph over these stresses and more.

STRESS
and the
HEALTHY FAMILY

DOLORES CURRAN

HarperPaperbacks
A Division of HarperCollinsPublishers

I dedicate this book to the memory of my
brother Jim Fox who made my childhood
years more carefree and my adult years less
stressful by being the kind of person he was.
R.I.P.

HarperPaperbacks *A Division of* HarperCollins*Publishers*
        10 East 53rd Street, New York, N.Y. 10022

Copyright © 1985 by Dolores Curran
All rights reserved. No part of this book may be used or
reproduced in any manner whatsoever without written
permission of the publisher, except in the case of brief
quotations embodied in critical articles and reviews. For
information address HarperCollins*Publishers,*
10 East 53rd Street, New York, N.Y. 10022.

Previous editions of this book were published by Winston
Press in 1985 and by Harper & Row in 1987.

First HarperPaperbacks printing: April 1993

Printed in the United States of America

HarperPaperbacks and colophon are trademarks of
HarperCollins*Publishers*

10 9 8 7 6 5 4 3 2 1

Contents

Introduction

Stress and the Healthy Family is not intended to be a how-to book as much as a "how-they" book. In it, I attempt to identify the ten most common everyday stresses families face today and show how some families deal with them effectively and how others do not. I won't be discussing extraordinary stresses such as severe illness, divorce, and death, although these will be touched upon at times. Rather, we will be looking at ordinary stresses like spouses who refuse to talk or listen, more month than money at times, and children's behavior and misbehavior.

After months of studying families, I hope to share with readers how families who deal well with ordinary stresses function so that those who don't can peek into others' family lives and see what's going on that might be useful to them when an everyday stress tests their family fabric.

In an earlier book, *Traits of a Healthy Family,* I identified fifteen positive traits most commonly found in healthy families. While studying these families, I was struck by their ability to handle everyday stresses in a competent and confident manner, stresses which often disrupt other families. Although families with a preponderance of positive traits are likely to handle normal stresses more effectively, they do not necessarily have fewer stresses or less overall stress. One feature stands out, however; healthy families recognize that stresses are a means of identifying family strengths. When a family experiences a stress, it is tested as a unit and learns to use its strengths and resources.

The healthy family, then, doesn't eliminate normal stress as much as it develops ways of dealing with stress. The reward in studying these families comes from the realization that family stresses can actually lead to family strengths.

When a healthy family faces a stress, such as a bad report card, it develops creative techniques, flexible rules, and mutual support, all of which strengthen existing resources and silently tell the family that it is capable of handling an even greater stress. The skills and resources developed fatten the family bank account of strengths, and even though the report card incident may have been looked upon as a problem, many such families speak of an earlier stress as "good for the family."

While I refer to these stresses throughout the book as normal, ordinary, or everyday, I don't want to minimize their fundamental role in fostering satisfying and pleasant family life. Family scholars use the terms *functional* and *dysfunctional* to describe families. The functional family is one who, when faced with a stress, draws upon its resources to meet that stress and often becomes a stronger family as a result of conquering it.

A dysfunctional family is one who cannot dredge up enough resources to cope with a stress and as a result allows the stress to further strain or even fragment the family. But it doesn't require a catastrophic stress to create a dysfunctional family. A pileup of little everyday stresses can do it, with each one further weakening an already faltering unit. Probably more marriages suffer from loss of communication than from loss of health, from disagreement about how to spend money than from insufficient money, and from overscheduled calendars than from an extramarital affair.

One of the cruelest paradoxes of family stress is revealed by the family who gears up to meet large, unexpected, and overwhelming stresses but falls victim to predictable, everyday stresses. I worked with a military family like this. The family endured and overcame major stresses like frequent moves, temporary single parenting, a two-year stint in Vietnam, having babies in foreign lands, living in dense base housing with insufficient monies in an area where Americans were unpopular, and a teenage drug addiction. But it fell apart upon retirement. The husband and wife could deal with the extraordinary stresses of twenty-five years, but their marriage could not handle ordinary ones like whether she should go to work when he wanted her free to spend time with him or even how to fill their days after a lifetime of regimentation. I report sadly that this marriage did not last.

Yet, at one point this was a functioning family immensely capable of developing skills and resources to meet the demands of a stressful time. Why these resources were not there at retirement concerns all of us, regardless of family strength, because we don't know what lies ahead to test us or whether we will have the strengths, skills, and relationships to deal with potential stress if it occurs.

Because a family unit changes constantly as parents and children develop and grow, stresses also change. Some, however, are predictable, like the retirement stresses experienced by the military couple just described. We don't have to fear these stresses if we anticipate them and prepare for them. To help us do this, I will present the seven stages of family life along with the most commonly experienced stresses in each stage as part of this book.

Because we are also living in a time of a significant value and culture shift, in which issues like women working and men diapering are surfacing as stresses in the family, I am including an interpretation of this changing value system, which may help couples and families better understand what is happening to them as a result of outside pressures.

I am deeply indebted to the 660 respondents who shared the top stresses in their family-life experience and to those healthy families who allowed me to invade their privacy, ask questions, and observe their skills in dealing with normal family stresses. Without such respondents and families, this book could not have been written. My own family life is richer for what I have learned from others, and I am convinced the family lives of readers will profit also if I do my work properly and convey accurately the skills and strengths I discovered in families who deal effectively with everyday stress. There are thousands of them out there, and they have much to teach us about healthy family life in a stressful society.

I am also indebted to Miriam Frost, an extraordinary editor, who minimized my stress in turning out this book.

Several years ago when I was facing a September deadline with *Traits of a Healthy Family,* life around our home was predictably stressful. During August my teenage children stepped in and ran the household while I wrote from dawn to dark. One evening as I prepared to sink into bed at my new bedtime of 10:00 P.M., my college-aged daughter said with a sly grin, "Just think, Mom, someday you can write a sequel and call it *Straits of a Healthy Family.*"

I've thought of her title several times while working on this book. It has a certain ring to it. But like most stresses in the family, the deadline passed, and I learned once again that stress doesn't always lead to straits in family life, although it may seem to at times.

1

Family Stress—
Inevitable but Surmountable

*"I come home from work after a day filled with deci-
sions and deadlines. All I want is to sit in a relatively
quiet atmosphere with my wife and kids and recoup.
Instead I get phone messages, a harrassed wife, fighting
kids, and a fast dinner because there's always a game or
meeting to go to right now. Am I asking too much? Is
this kind of family stress inevitable and insurmountable
today?"*

—Thirty-six-year-old husband
and father of three

Inevitable, yes. Insurmountable, no. All families live with
stress and generally share the same everyday stressors—
finances, calendars, children's behaviors— but some families
develop structures and skills that deal with normal stress
while others succumb to it. Some learn to control family
stress; others allow stress to control their family lives.

Family stress, a relatively new phrase in town, is the latest
in a progression of stress and burnout syndromes that began
to show up a couple of decades ago with a syndrome called
executive stress. Executive stress was first perceived in corporate circles, and it achieved prestigious status. If one didn't
have an ulcer, high blood pressure, or angina, one simply
wasn't working up to potential. But while executive stress has
received a great deal of attention, family stress has been
largely ignored until recently.

A 1984 news story in a Denver daily, *The Rocky Mountain News*, told of a young couple in which the wife gave birth to premature twins who suffered from vision, lung, and heart problems. Six months later, the mother came down with Guillain-Barre syndrome, which affects the nerve endings and requires long months of hospital care. While she was hospitalized, her husband worked his regular shift as a delivery truck driver from 2:30 A.M. to 11:00 A.M., visited and cared for her three times a day at the hospital, checked the progress of the twins at home with round-the-clock nurses, and visited an older preschooler who had been sent to live with a nearby aunt.

But the gist of the story—the point that was featured—was that he had not allowed all this to interfere with his job. "He does not carry his personal problems to work," said his boss. "I called him in here just to tell him how much I appreciated that. We talk about it continuously. When you see somebody like that, still performing their job, that's somebody to look up to."[1]

I admit I find it easier to look up to the young father than to his boss. This story points out rather dramatically the dichotomy between the way our society has viewed work-related stress and the way it has seen family-related stress. The young man was congratulated for not bringing his catastrophic family stresses to work. That would not have been acceptable. But we have accepted and expected work stresses to be brought home.

We know that spillover of family stress into the workplace jeopardizes the job. We also know that spillover of work stress into the home jeopardizes healthy family life, yet we accept and approve the latter. "Don't tell me about your sick child" is an unspoken yet understood message from employers who see little contradiction when they ask the same employee to work overtime. We can be sure that the parent who readily agrees to the extra work will be seen as more promotable than the one who replies, "Gee, I'm sorry, but I want to spend some time with my family this weekend."

Stress which is acknowledged and even expected in the workplace is often demeaned and denounced in the homeplace. Families aren't supposed to be places of stress; they are supposed to be places of peace and harmony in which we recoup from the pressures of the outside world and gather new energy to put back into our jobs. Whether or not the family ever really was that "haven in a heartless world," as tradition has long revered, the ideal has strong roots in our culture.

And this idealized view of family produces great guilt in parents who live with everyday family stresses. Rather than acknowledging such pressures as valid, we submerge them and feel as if we have failed as spouses and parents when they erupt.

I recall the time I ran into an acquaintance at the supermarket and asked her how things were going. It was the wrong question. Her eyes filled with tears as she confided that she had just been severely berated by her child's scoutmaster for forgetting an important den meeting. "You mothers want us to do everything for your children, but you don't even care enough to see that your kids get here," the scoutmaster had charged. She had tried to apologize and explain to him the circumstances of the day she had forgotten the meeting, but he had already hung up on her.

I listened to her tale of self-recrimination. On that day of the meeting, she had four after-school activities to which she chauffeured various children, had a sick child at home, and had unexpected houseguests. Small wonder she forgot a den meeting.

Yet, in the eyes of the den leader and in her own eyes, she had failed—failed her son, failed his pack, and failed in motherhood. This woman was a victim of family stress. She was totally dedicated to keeping her overinvolved family running smoothly, her home clean and attractive, and her volunteer work exemplary. When I spoke with her, she was suffering from painfully damaged self-esteem because she had not lived up to society's expectation of her role as parent.

The fact is that many of the stresses which families face are rooted in work patterns, school policies, church attitudes, and community expectations. All of these stresses come to roost in the home and create family problems that rebound into society.

A church attitude that says a mother should not work outside the home puts stress on mothers who *must* work. A business attitude that says a father's primary duty is to work increases stress in a family that wants equal time for fathering. A school climate that lacks effective discipline causes great stress in families who prize responsible behavior in their children.

Because family stress is spilling over into society, it is beginning to receive some attention. Time pressures on families in which both parents work are affecting the job performances of these men and women. At least 75 percent of the *Fortune* 500 companies now have marriage and family professionals on staff because employees *are* bringing problems to work, and these problems are family-oriented. Schools, which have long insisted that a child's achievement is based more on parent motivation and support than on curricula and teaching methods, are beginning to offer practical parenting education programs. And churches that inherit family breakdown are beginning to focus as much on ministering to the family at home as on getting the family to church. These actions are creating new hope and excitement in the midst of a cultural myth that the family is dying. To the contrary, the family is finally beginning to get the attention it deserves from the institutions which are set up to serve it. Instead of viewing the family solely as a unit which exists to make society richer, we are recognizing that a productive society goes hand in hand with healthy families and that our institutions have a responsibility for making family life richer.

Family and society are interdependent. What enriches one enriches the other. What damages one damages the other. Instead of using the popular convenience of scapegoating families for society's failures, we are starting to take a hard look at institutional responsibilities for supporting families by reducing the stresses and pressures brought about by policies and attitudes long honored in our history.

Once we recognize that family stress is as predictable and as valid as executive stress and professional burnout, we can apply the same kind of principles and efforts in relieving it. Fortunately, this has already begun. An explosion in research the past five years on what constitutes major family stress and how to alleviate it is sifting down into institutional programs. A glance at any community college, adult education, or church brochure finds courses and workshops on family-related issues unimagined ten years ago.

In just one suburban community adult education schedule, I found the following: Family Fitness; Managing Personal Stress; Understanding Non-verbal Communication; Adjustment to Divorce; Tackling the Terrible Two's; Assertiveness Training for Teens; Overcoming Test Anxiety; Living with a Family Computer; Caring for Children with Special Needs; and Creative Discipline. Offerings like these acknowledge predictable stresses and give families permission to own them, but they also go a step further, for they promise help and hope which at one time were nonexistent.

Family stress differs from other forms of stress because of the interrelationships involved. If one member is under stress, it affects the entire family. A severely ill child, a workaholic father, a perfectionist mother, houseguests, neighbors—only one of these is required to create an intensely stressful climate in the home, a climate which produces a ripple effect on individual lives.

According to *Time*, stress can be responsible for physical illnesses within the family as well. "Perhaps the most significant new discovery about stress is its deleterious effect on the immune system. Researchers have discovered that the body's production of its own cancer-fighting cells, including natural killer cells, T-lymphocytes and macrophages, is inhibited by chronic stress."[2] So when members of highly stressed families complain, "You're giving me a headache," or, "You're driving me crazy," they may not be completely exaggerating.

One image family scholars use to help families understand the nature of stress is that of a hanging mobile. Imagine a family suspended in midair by fine nylon cord. When all is going well, the figures are in balance. The family mobile can be thrown out of balance in two ways: from within the family unit by either normal or catastrophic stresses and from outside the family by societal pressures. If a new baby, a stepparent, or an elderly parent is added to the family, that member creates an imbalance for a period of time, and the mobile becomes shaky. If a child goes off to college, or parents divorce, or a family member dies, the family unit is even more violently shaken.

A new baby, for example, is a normal family stress which results in temporary sleepless nights, less shared spousal time, and displacement of the youngest as baby. Everyone in the family is forced to change, at least temporarily. New behaviors and adjustments come into play, and family resources and strengths eventually determine the length of time it takes for the family to get into balance again.

The second way the family mobile becomes unsettled is from outside pressures. Just as wind or vibrations set a mobile dancing, so too can outside stresses like inflation, a move, or adolescent peer pressures upset the fine balance within a family. A too-familiar experience of this comes when a major industry shuts down and hundreds of employees are thrown out of work. Stresses of unemployment compound stresses already existing within the family and often paralyze it.

I spoke with the pastor of a church in a community that suffered severe economic depression when an automotive plant closed. He expressed dismay at the disruption it caused within family life. "If you told me a year ago that some of these strong families were only as strong as the breadwinner's weekly paycheck, I would have disagreed," he said. "But now I realize how fragile and dependent families are upon the economy." The truth of his statement is borne out in my research. *The number one stress reported by respondents has to do with economics, financing, and budgeting.*

So families find themselves negotiating change within and without simultaneously. In some families, when all is going well within, they are able to gather their resources and deal with major outside stresses; other families fall apart when an outside pressure threatens, even though their individual unit has been okay. It is helpful for us to scrutinize families who handle stress effectively and try to discover what is going on inside the family dynamic that enables them to control their stress level rather than allow it to control and fragment them.

Here are some reactions of families who handle stress effectively:

1. They tend to recognize that the stress is temporary, maybe even positive.
2. They work together on solutions to minimize the stress, which, in turn, strengthens family skills.
3. They develop new rules such as prioritizing time and sharing responsibilities.
4. They expect some stress as a normal part of family life without considering themselves failures.
5. They feel good about themselves for dealing effectively with the new stress.

Families who do *not* deal with normal stresses as effectively show the following characteristics in stressful situations:

1. They feel guilty for permitting a stress to exist.
2. They look for a place to lay blame rather than for a solution to the problem.
3. They give in to stress and give up trying to master it.
4. They focus on family problems rather than on family strengths.
5. They feel weaker rather than stronger after experiencing normal stress.
6. They grow to dislike family life as a result of the buildup of stresses.

In their book, *Families: What Makes Them Work?* family scholars David Olson and Hamilton McCubbin discuss research linking stress and family life. After examining the research, they state unequivocally, "Satisfied families were not stressed families, and families under stress were, indeed, dissatisfied. The results are clear and consistent that couples under stress are equally dissatisfied with their marriages, with their family lives, and with the quality of their lives."[3]

But we need to realize that some stress is good. It's an important element of mental health. A depressed person blocks out stress with sleep, drugs, alcohol, or even work. If we didn't have positive stress—eustress—we wouldn't get energized to meet deadlines or to finish what we start. In truth, parents often wish a particular child were a bit more stressed and less relaxed in daily life responsibilities. A classic parent refrain I hear is, "If Jeremy showed a little more stress, I'd show less."

Georgia Witkin-Lanoil, a clinical psychologist and author of *Female Stress Syndrome,* claims, "You have to have some stress. The only people without any stress are dead people. Stress is staying busy. It can be stimulating. The key is control. As long as you have some feeling of control, stress is beneficial."[4]

If some stress is good, then why isn't more stress better? Because there is a point at which eustress becomes distress and interferes with the healthy functioning of individuals and families. This point varies in families.

I define family dis-stress as *a condition that exists when family life gets out of control.* Familiar symptoms of a *constantly stressful family* include

- a constant sense of urgency and hurry; no time to release and relax
- tension that underlies and causes sharp words, sibling fighting, misunderstandings
- a mania to escape—to one's room, car, garage, away
- feelings of frustration over not getting things done
- a feeling that time is passing too quickly; children are growing up too fast
- a nagging desire for a simpler life; constant talk about times that were or will be simpler
- little "me" or couple time
- a pervasive sense of guilt for not being and doing everything to and for all the people in one's life

All families experience these symptoms at times, but some families live with them at peak level constantly. When this occurs, negative stress takes over and becomes the prevailing mood.

It was to this kind of mood the father in my opening paragraph was referring. His poignant dream of family life as a haven of love and leisure is voiced by thousands of parents today, men and women alike. But his naked question, "Is this kind of family stress inevitable?" disclosed his frustration and inability to get family life and personal expectations under reasonable control. And when stress dominated his family life, he wanted to believe that the stress couldn't be controlled.

It can. Thousands of families have proved that they can be successful employees, active participants in community life, and good spouses and parents while enjoying family as a place to refresh and renew. However, they operate differently from families who suffer or become dysfunctional because of normal, everyday stresses. Let's move on to those stresses and see how healthy families handle them.

2

Looking at the
Top Ten Everyday Stresses

"Completing this survey was very stressful for us and led to quite a discussion. I had difficulty narrowing the number of stresses down to 10, while my husband couldn't choose more than three. I was surprised and upset that we couldn't even agree on the same stresses in our family."

—Thirty-two-year-old wife
and mother of two

The greatest surprise in my research on stress and family life came from the discovery that members of the same family were not in agreement on what was stressful to their family. The wife's reaction above was by no means atypical. A couple in one of my parenting workshops agreed to complete the stress survey, choosing the ten most stressful situations in their life together. As instructed, they studied the list of choices individually and made their selections. Then they shared the completed surveys with one another before they returned them to me. I was grateful that we were on break because their agitation with one another became noticeable in their voice level, fast exchange of words, and flushed faces. Feeling a bit responsible and wanting to spare them some embarrassment because the group was beginning to notice, I wandered over and said, "I hate to be guilty of creating stress where there wasn't any, especially through a stress survey. Want to rip it up?"

They looked up guiltily and then laughed. "Can we talk about this when we regather as a group?" she asked. "There are some items here that I think Jack should find stressful and he doesn't. I'd like to know if this is common in other couples as well."

We did talk about the survey, and disagreement between husbands and wives was common—a pattern I came to recognize early in my initial research. I realized that determining the top ten everyday stresses in family life was much more complex than I had originally believed. I discovered that the stresses selected differed particularly among three basic groups: *married men, married women,* and *single mothers.* (There simply aren't enough fathers who remain single and assume the role of primary caregiver to draw valid conclusions on their family stress level.) So I realized that a major part of my research and book would have to deal with the *differences* in perceived stresses as well as the *similarities.* No tidy little agreement between spouses or even between married women and single mothers emerged to make the job easier.

My initial survey included forty-five stressful situations commonly found in family life. I asked 210 respondents in four geographically scattered areas to rank the stresses and selected the top twenty-five for my final survey instrument. Then I refined my original survey instrument, dropping the twenty least-selected stressors and adding a request for information on gender, marital status, ages of children, and family income. I sent this final survey instrument to 450 men and women (including 169 couples, 239 married women, and 42 single mothers).

At this point, I invite readers to take pen in hand and name their family stresses before reading those most commonly named by the 450 men and women who responded to my final survey.

A SURVEY ON COMMON STRESSES IN THE FAMILY

Listed below are twenty-five situations that can lead to an increase of stress in normal family life. *Please check the ten* that create or have created the most stress in your family life. *After you have checked these ten, please number them one through ten* in order of degree, one being the most stressful and ten being the least.

_____ Communicating with children
_____ Economics/finances/budgeting
_____ Guilt for not accomplishing more
_____ Housekeeping standards
_____ Insufficient couple time
_____ Insufficient family playtime
_____ Insufficient "me" time
_____ Overscheduled family calendar
_____ Overvoluntarism
_____ Unhappiness with work situation
_____ Children's behavior/discipline/sibling fighting
_____ Family member(s) feeling unappreciated
_____ Lack of shared responsibility in the family
_____ Self-image/self-esteem/feelings of unattractiveness
_____ Spousal relationship (communication, friendship, sex)
_____ Teen behaviors (communication, music, friends, church, school)
_____ Television
_____ Perfectionism
_____ New baby
_____ Neighbors
_____ Moving
_____ In-laws
_____ Holidays
_____ Dieting
_____ Health/illness

Please do not sign your name,
but this information will be helpful:

_____ Male   _____ Female

___ Married
___ Divorced
___ Widowed
___ Never married

Ages of children _____

Family income   _____ Less than $10,000
                 _____ $10,000-20,000
                 _____ $20,000-30,000
                 _____ $30,000-40,000
                 _____ Over $40,000

Readers might be interested in the twenty stresses which were *not* highly ranked on the original instrument and were subsequently dropped from the final survey. They include

retirement
widowhood
drugs/alcohol
houseguests
nuclear and environmental fears
older parents
church and school activities
family vacations
remarriage
relationship with former spouse
summers
unsatisfactory housing
two-paycheck family
organized sports/activities
change in work patterns
homework/school/grades
religious differences
weekends
predinner hour
unemployment

Some of these, of course, are everyday stresses, and some, like remarriage and unemployment, are major stresses, so comparing them with items like the predinner hour seems like comparing the proverbial apples and oranges. But apples and oranges are what family life is all about. As I indicated earlier, probably as many families have suffered from predinner-hour stress as from unemployment stress. Indeed, they may garner the resources to meet stress fallout from unemployment but capitulate to that most dreaded hour in the family day—the predinner hour. We don't call it the cocktail hour by coincidence.

This is not to say that the above stresses are minimal and not worthy of our attention. Many create severe stress levels in families where they exist, but they do not exist as commonly in families as some of the other stressors. Drugs and alcohol, for example, can create a life of misery and violence for all members of a family, but as widespread as this stress is, there are still more families who do not have it, so it is predictable that other situations would be chosen as more generally stressful.

The following table shows the ten situations most often selected by married men, married women, and single mothers as being stressful in their families.

TOP STRESSES IN ORDER OF PRIORITY

Total Group
1. Economics/finances/budgeting
2. Children's behavior/discipline/sibling fighting
3. Insufficient couple time
4. Lack of shared responsibility in the family
5. Communicating with children
6. Insufficient "me" time
7. Guilt for not accomplishing more
8. Spousal relationship (communication, friendship, sex)
9. Insufficient family playtime
10. Overscheduled family calendar

Female Married
1. Economics/finances/budgeting
2. Lack of shared responsibility in the family
3. Insufficient couple time
4. Children's behavior/discipline/sibling fighting
5. Housekeeping standards
6. Insufficient "me" time
7. Guilt for not accomplishing more
8. Insufficient family playtime
9. Spousal relationship (communication, friendship, sex)
10. Self-image/self-esteem/feelings of unattractiveness

Male Married
1. Economics/finances/budgeting
2. Insufficient couple time
3. Communicating with children
4. Children's behavior/discipline/sibling fighting
5. Spousal relationship (communication, friendship, sex)
6. Overscheduled family calendar
7. Insufficient "me" time
8. Unhappiness with work situation
9. Insufficient family playtime
10. Television

Single Mothers
1. Economics/finances/budgeting
2. Guilt for not accomplishing more
3. Insufficient "me" time
4. Self-image/self-esteem/feelings of unattractiveness
5. Children's behavior/discipline/sibling fighting
6. Unhappiness with work situation
7. Housekeeping standards
8. Communicating with children
9. Insufficient family playtime
10. Lack of shared responsibility in the family

My findings parallel other family stress studies, in particular the Martha's Vineyard Child Health Survey, which is believed by stress experts to be the most sophisticated and comprehensive survey undertaken of behavioral disorders among the children of an entire community. Preliminary results show that among families reporting chronic, stress-producing difficulties, the most prevalent worry was financial security, followed by housing, work, marriage, and health problems.[1]

When we realize that we began with a possible forty-five stressors in family life and ultimately agree upon only four when we combine the major categories—married men, married women, and single mothers—we can see that much of our stress identification stems from a personal bias. This bias often conflicts with that of our mate, which, in turn, tends to create more stress. The wife in my opening anecdote was more stressed after completing the survey simply because her husband did not share her stresses. She realized, perhaps for the first time, that he was assigning areas of family stress to her which she felt should be shared by him.

Gender Role Differences

Several intriguing questions arise from this survey information. Of the couples (169) who responded, the husband and the wife each completed a separate survey. Yet four of the ten, or nearly half, the stresses selected were different within the same family. What is this telling us? Why such disparity? These couples share the same income, the same children, and, presumably, the same age and educational levels. Are the children in these families difficult to communicate with or not? Husbands say yes, and wives say no. Are housekeeping standards a problem? Wives say yes, and husbands say no. Is television a stress? Surprisingly to me, husbands say yes, and wives say no. Is lack of shared responsibility in the family a stress? Wives say yes, husbands say no.

When I undertook the writing of this book, I had little intention of getting into gender perceptions and roles because I didn't anticipate their significance in family stress, but my research indicates they cannot be ignored. Obviously, husbands perceive different stresses than wives within the same family unit.

Single mothers tend to combine the stresses of married fathers and mothers, naming the typical male stresses of unhappiness with work situation and communicating with children, which were not in the top ten named by their married counterparts, while also naming housekeeping standards and guilt for not accomplishing more, which were selected by married women but not by men. Clearly, this pattern indicates the dual role of the single mother trying to combine both roles of father and mother in one.

Guilt seems curiously absent from the men's list. Even though men listed all four kinds of time pressures as stresses, they are the only group who didn't name "guilt for not accomplishing more" as a major stress.

Are women basically more guilt-prone, or have we assigned the task of achieving a smooth-running, relaxed family life to women? Probably both, given our tradition and cultural conditioning. Perhaps if I had included "guilt for not earning more money" as a choice, men would have reported more guilt. From their responses, single mothers seem to be living with the most guilt of any group.

Another indication that gender plays a big role in family stress lies in self-image. Thirty-four percent of married women and 52 percent of single mothers reported self-image, self-esteem, and feelings of unattractiveness as a stress while only 1 percent (yes, that's one percent) of the men did so. This is such a significant variance that we need to look at it closely.

Are women in families that deal less effectively with everyday stress actually less capable and less attractive than their husbands or than women in healthy families? No. Do they place higher expectations on themselves? Perhaps. I will deal with this more fully in the chapters ahead because self-esteem is foundational to healthy relationships and families are places of relationship.

I was startled at first to find that only men as a group named television as a top stress, because one of the complaints I hear most often from wives in workshops is the amount of time their husbands spend in front of the set. But I now realize stress occurs because men want to spend *more* time viewing television, particularly sports, naming it as their top "me" time activity, while women tend to view TV as an obstacle to more couple time and more family playtime.

Actual Versus Perceived Stresses

Obviously, from the above research we begin to sense that stress in the family is not a simple matter of listing stressors and getting rid of them, which is precisely what most of us try to do when a stress erupts in family life. Getting rid of the television set, for instance, may relieve a particular wife's stress, but it will increase her husband's if he uses it for "me" time relaxation.

In order to relieve the stress created by television in such a family, we have to look at the difference between *actual* and *perceived* stress, which is related to expectations on the part of the family members.

Let's take a hypothetical family in which Mom is unhappy because although her dream family spends Sunday afternoons sharing some activity—a day at the beach or at Grandma's, or playing volleyball—her real family is uninterested in sharing that activity. Dad is unhappy because he perceives Sunday as *his* time, the only time during the week when he can sink into a chair in front of the TV and lose himself in football. The kids are unhappy because they want to spend Sunday playing with other kids in the neighborhood.

Is television, then, an actual stressor or a perceived one? Even if there were no television in the home, stress would remain because each family member perceives the use of time and expectations differently. What pleases one member is bound to displease another.

Let's say Mom "wins," plans an outing, and prepares the food and the activity, only to find her family unappreciative and uncooperative. It's a familiar situation, one depicted in the classic cartoon of the family camping and one of the children saying, "Tell us again we're having fun, Mom."

Or let's say Dad "wins" and the rest of the family stands around watching him watch television—another familiar situation that has spawned literally hundreds of cartoons and jokes.

Or let's say the children "win" and the family capitulates to their wishes for the day, a third familiar situation in which most family free time centers around children's needs and activities. Parents in such families tend to enshrine the children's activities, granting them primacy over parent needs and couple activities. Eventually, this can diminish the couple relationship to the point of nonexistence and is one of the chief causes of empty nest shock—the point at which the couple realizes it no longer has a relationship to share without their children around.

In our hypothetical family, then, television is not the actual stressor but a perceived stressor. The actual stressor is more fundamental: who owns free time? The individual? The couple? The family? The employer? Or even yellow waxy buildup? (In some families, free time is viewed as the time to clean and repair the home or car.)

Is free time in the family my time, our time, or their time? It depends on our expectations, and these expectations come from a variety of sources— one's childhood, media images of family, and individual perceptions of rights.

The wife in one family I worked with came from a strong southern Baptist background in which her childhood family spent all of Sunday in church and on family-related activities. She expected the same when she married. Her husband came from a family in which individual activities and time were highly valued, and he expected to use Sunday on his hobby of restoring old cars. Their kids' expectations came from their suburban peers, and they wanted to spend Sunday "cruising the mall" with other kids.

Before this family could deal with the "stress" of Sunday, they had to examine and share their unspoken expectations and come to some compromise or collaboration, accepting the fact that there was no answer that was going to please all of the members every Sunday.

Here is the dynamic that goes on inside healthy families: They develop attitudes which say, "I care enough about your expectations and needs to give up some of mine." Idealistic, yes, but not overly so. The solution demands communication skills often absent in the not-so-healthy families wherein individuals tend to rigidify and assert their own rights rather than compromise and recognize the rights of others.

Nowhere is this situation more obvious than in the number one stress named by all three groups: economics/finances/budgeting. If the actual stress was merely insufficient money, financial stress would appear in lower income levels only.

But it was named first in *all* income categories, those over $40,000 as well as those under $10,000. Clearly, the quantity of money is not the stress as much as expectations on how money is to be spent. These expectations spring from individual roots and are often unexamined and undiscussed until they appear in the form of overspending or scrimping, loans or getting by without, credit cards or paying only with cash, allowances or no allowances, and, ultimately, tension over who owns paycheck power.

Families on *all* income levels experience disagreements over money to some degree because they bring different attitudes toward money into the family unit. Because their individual expectations are different, their perceptions of money as a stress are different.

The wife who views an unexpected windfall like a Christmas bonus as money to be spent but who has a husband who views it as money to be salted away will name money as a stress. It isn't. Here, the stress is the inability to talk about the situation in a way that takes the other's expectations into account. Each tries to convince the other that he or she is "right," while in healthy relationships, each partner tries to understand and respond to the other's expectations while articulating his or her own. Such a couple may end up spending part and saving part of the unexpected windfall, with both partners somewhat satisfied, while the couple who acquiesces to one partner's preference may well end up permitting a potential pleasure to become a source of tension.

* * *

In dealing with stress, healthy couples tend to seek solutions, and less communicative couples tend to place blame—on the other partner, on the children, on work, or on society in general. That is why we must begin our scrutiny of family stress with the spousal relationship, although it is not the top stress selected in our survey. It is out of the couple relationship that the other stressors spring, and it is the couple relationship that determines the ability of the family to deal with other everyday pressures.

Let's look at what goes on in the spousal relationship within healthy families that enables them to deal effectively with stressors like money, children, and time.

3

The Couple Relationship

The couple relationship was named as a stress by 43 percent of married men, 34 percent of married women, and 14 percent of single mothers. Overall, couple relationship was named as the eighth top stress.

* * *

"I notice that when things are going well between us, other pressures disappear. But if we're not clicking, even the cat becomes a stress."

—Forty-one-year-old husband

"Clicking" is an apt word to use in looking at the basic factor in controlling everyday stress in the family. What makes couples click? What goes on inside the healthy spousal relationship that enables some couples to deal more effectively with time, money, work, and children than others? In an attempt to isolate commonalities among stress-effective couples, I interviewed and studied thirty-two couples and eight single parents identified as healthy by professionals who responded to my earlier research for *Traits of a Healthy Family*. Certain attitudes and characteristics surfaced among these families that give a clue to the dynamic which enables them to control normal stress well in their families.

Because the word *couple* in this book is necessary in discussing the two-parent family structure, I have used it frequently. However, the discussion applies to single-parent families as well. I suggest single parents substitute the word *family* where couple is used because in the single-parent family, the couple interaction usually transfers into a parent/children interaction, a parent/grandparent interaction, or a parent/friend interaction. I leave it to the single-parent reader to substitute whichever grouping is most appropriate. At times, of course, the use of couple is fitting for the single parent if the former spouse is involved in the issue under discussion.

The following are five characteristics of couples who handle stress in a healthy way:

- They view stress as a normal part of family life.
- They share feelings as well as words.
- They develop conflict-resolution skills and creative coping skills.
- They make use of support people and systems.
- They are adaptable.

1. The healthy couple views stress as a normal part of family life.

Healthy couples do not equate family life with perfection. Their expectations and goals are frequently lower than those of other couples. These couples don't link problems with self-failure, but rather anticipate stresses like children's behavior and occasional disagreements over money as a normal part of married life, and they develop ways of coping that are both traditional and unique.

Expectations in marriage play a foundational role in a couple's satisfaction with marriage. For example, if he expects her to be satisfied with his role as a good provider while finding his primary need for intimacy satisfied in his work, and she expects him to find his primary intimacy needs satisfied within the family, stress is predictable. Family scholars are bending their attention to this expectation factor in marriage to predict marital satisfaction. A recent paper delivered before the National Council on Family Relations provides an instrument to measure the degree of contrast between couple expectations in their relationship and complaints about the relationship.[1] If such an instrument becomes commonplace, couples may eventually be able to name their expectations before marriage rather than presume they share the same ones.

Couples often have very different expectations of what marriage and marriage roles mean. A woman quoted in a *Woman's Day* article on "The Myth of the 50/50 Marriage" said, "When we got married I was expected to stay home and be ready to be 'together' with my husband at a moment's notice. We had many arguments when I wanted to go back to school for a degree in social work; he deeply believed it was an insult to his masculinity and pride to have a wife who worked. Then it was OK with him if I worked—in fact, he was secretly very proud of me—as long as I didn't make much money or question the priority of his career." This couple had to renegotiate their expectations in order to deal with the normal stresses change brought. Later on, she ruefully reported, "Now I think he'd be happy to let me support him!"[2]

Couples with a strong spousal relationship expect change as part of growth and expect stress to result as part of this change. The first skill, then, in dealing with family stress springs from the couple's expectations and their ability to express them to one another.

2. The healthy couple shares feelings as well as words.
"In a survey, 5,000 German husbands and wives were asked how often they talked to each other. After two years of marriage, most managed two or three minutes of conversation at breakfast, more than 20 minutes over dinner, and a few minutes in bed. By the sixth year, the total was down to 10 minutes a day. A state of 'almost total speechlessness' was reached by the eighth year of marriage."[3]

Lack of communication is not an exclusively German phenomenon. "Whenever my husband is in a deep gloom, I have to play search and destroy," said an American wife. "Why won't he share his feelings? The more I search, the gloomier he gets."

It's a familiar complaint, one that family educator David Thomas and I decided to address at a couple workshop in which we separated husbands and wives and asked each group to list what they perceived as major problems with communication in their marriage. Here is what we heard from the twenty-two men:

- She demands immediate answers. I want to think about it for awhile.
- She always looks for hidden meanings. She reads in meanings that aren't there.
- She is never satisfied with what I tell her. I don't like cross-examinations.
- She belabors the subject—wants all the details. Her stories take detours. Why can't she get to the point?
- She can't separate the issue from the person. She thinks, "If you disagree with my view, then you don't love me."
- My homemaker wife is always saying (sometimes wordlessly), "Notice me. Tell me I'm worthwhile." It's unnerving.
- She brings unrelated issues into the argument.
- Feminism is a part of every discussion. All issues turn into gender justice issues.
- My wife has a great need to control conversation and events.
- She interrupts me. She tends to break into whatever I say before I'm finished.
- She desires more to be understood than to understand.

Here is what the twenty-two wives reported:

- He doesn't listen to full conversations or even sentences but judges immediately.
- He doesn't respect my opinion but hears it only when someone else says it.
- He won't risk confrontation. If I complain, he doesn't answer, and I feel like a nonperson.
- Reminding is taken as nagging.
- His problems are major. Mine are insignificant and incessant.
- He gets angry when I interrupt for clarification, especially during his long stories.
- He doesn't listen—just pretends—and when I catch him at it, he gets angry.

- He won't share his true feelings, but they emerge heatedly later on.
- I share feelings and frustrations, but nothing happens.
- He won't fight. Anything I say will be the "wrong" thing.
- If something goes wrong in his life, he makes me feel as if I have failed.
- He can't share the deep feelings of intimacy I need.
- He's too busy for communication. (said by several women)
- When he's mad at the dog or car, why is it my fault and why does he take it out on me?
- He can't admit he's wrong.
- Why tell me about the kids' misbehavior? Why doesn't he do something about it? Instead, he tattles.
- He ignores me all day and then wants quick and playful sex at night. I don't want sex without attention first.

A postdoctoral degree in marriage counseling is not required to recognize that these are basically the same issues viewed from opposing perspectives:

- She takes too long to get to the point—he interrupts.
- She's always looking for hidden meanings—he won't share his feelings.
- She can't separate the issue from the person—he won't risk confrontation.

A careful reading of these complaints reveals that couples need to communicate on a *feeling* level as well as a *verbal* level, and here's where healthy couples have greater skill than other couples. They don't depend on a "grocery list" level of communication to sustain their relationship: "Is there gas in the car?" "Your mother called." "Tim pitched a no-hitter."

When I interviewed the couples who communicated effectively, I was struck by the many nonthreatening techniques they developed to get in touch with their own and their partners' feelings. "I learned early in our marriage not to say, 'What's bothering you?'" one woman said. "His answer was always, 'Nothing.' And if I pushed he became angry or silent. One day I told him, 'I feel so lonely when something's bothering you and you won't tell me . . . like I've failed.' And I meant it.

"He was astonished at my reaction. He said, 'I don't want you to feel like that. The reason I don't tell you my worries is because I don't want to worry you.'

"Here we were, both concerned about the other's feelings but I was accusing him of being unfeeling and he was accusing me of intruding. I convinced him that hiding his feelings was more painful to me than any worry he could share. We agreed that when I felt he was shutting me out, I would say to him, 'I'm feeling lonely,' and he'd try to be more open. It's taken a long time for us but it works. Sometimes it's a risk, though."

Risk is a word we hear often from couples when they talk about feelings. "He won't risk confrontation." "I can't risk telling her." Yet, intimacy is built upon risk. It implies being able to risk one's vulnerability by sharing feelings that might not be acceptable to the other. When partners risk and there's belittlement or no response at all, another layer of protection is built around feelings. Some couples have such thick walls that the only time feelings emerge is in explosive anger.

In an article, "The Stresses of Intimacy," Michael Griffin writes, "If there is going to be deep intimacy, there will be stress. There can be no deep intimacy between a couple unless there is a great deal of fighting about what is important. Two people who care deeply about what is important to them are bound to come into conflict. If intimacy is the most important thing in life then the price must be paid to achieve this in conflict and struggle. But the rewards can be enormous."[4]

Love and intimacy don't come easily, however. We know how to work and how to cook because these skills were prized in an earlier economic model of family. We accepted honorable labels like the "hardworking man" and the "good little mother" as applied to husbands and wives. As a consequence, persons who fit such labels became enshrined as the underpinning of successful marriages.

Today we find ourselves seeking intimacy at its deepest level in a highly technological society, but we (particularly men) don't know how to be intimate. Intimacy is a skill to be learned and to share, and yet we're novices as far as understanding it. How often I hear a wife say, "He's a wonderful provider, a good father, and never unfaithful *but* . . . ," and then she indicates that they can't talk or share feelings.

Psychiatrist Harold Lief, director of the Institute for Marital and Sexual Health in Philadelphia, believes that many people never learn to recognize and express feelings. "Fearful of sounding foolish or of bruising another's feelings, they're also tongue-tied by the risks of exposing themselves, of being vulnerable, of getting hurt. It *is* scary," Dr. Lief concedes, "but, if you play it too safe, your relationship will suffer. In effect, every couple truly committed to staying together have to create a language, a special code of words, gestures and actions that only they fully understand."[5]

I found that many healthy couples create their own code. Certain words give permission to open up while others warn, "Stay away." A letter from a reader of an article I wrote on family communication caused me to reflect on fear and lack of adequate language. She wrote, "I just finished reading your article and just have to tell you how much I enjoyed it. I only wish my husband would read it. *I intend to cut it out and mail it to his office* and hope he will take the time to read it as we could benefit from it." What an obvious communication problem right there. She has to mail the article to his office to get his attention. Their level of communication has become so impersonalized that it takes place through the U.S. mail, even though they live together.

Rose DeWolf, author of *How to Raise Your Man*, says women often complain about communication but that they don't do anything about it. "Here's an example," she said. "I came home from the store the other day with six shopping bags, and I'm making this horrible rattling noise with them. And I'm thinking: 'There he is, sitting on the sofa reading. Why isn't he helping? I'm sure he hears me.' And then I say to myself: 'Rose, you nitwit, why do you assume he knows you want his help if you haven't asked him for it. He probably assumes you want to do it your way and don't want him messing in.' So I said, 'Hey, honey, can I have some help?'

-34-

And in three seconds flat, he's there helping with the bags. All I had to do was ask."[6]

Healthy, communicating couples use humor positively, not destructively. "When I want to be silly and he doesn't, Tom gives me a time-out sign and I know he's not in the mood for my silliness so I stifle it," said one wife. "How do you know when he's open to silliness?" I asked. "Oh, he usually screws up his face in a not-this-again grimace and I know it's okay. When we were first married, he could never be carefree or silly and I need that. But now he enjoys it, and we can break a lot of tension with a few good laughs together."

When couples begin to share feelings, they begin to become friends, not just spouses or lovers. This element of friendship is mentioned frequently by couples in good relationships. "We're good friends. We can talk about anything." Because most marriages begin with a sexual attraction rather than friendship, some couples never become good friends.

Being a good friend means being able to share ideas, activities, and feelings without being owned or judged. A line near the end of *Tootsie* reveals the dual nature of a good marital relationship. In the movie Dustin Hoffman pleads with Jessica Lange to resume their relationship as man and woman instead of two women. He says, "We've already proved we can be friends. That's the hard part."

I see a reluctance on the part of many young people today to cross the line from a friendship to a dating relationship. They realize that the nature of the relationship will change, and they don't want to jeopardize the friendship. It's a sad commentary on our cultural attitudes toward marriage—that spouses can't be friends.

I received a letter from a reader of my column who exhibits the loneliness found within many marriages. She wrote, "I am a 52-year-old woman married for almost 33 years and the mother of 4 grown children. I am wondering if I am one of a kind or if there are more women like myself who are married and yet feel 'unmarried.' I do not want to be divorced nor do I want an affair. Society, through workshops, seminars, meetings, et cetera, seems to deal with people only in regard to problems: death, divorce, terminal illness, mental and physical handicaps, alcoholism. I feel very lonely, unloved, unappreciated, and just seem 'to be here'—desperate for a loving, caring companion. I'm too old for the jet set and too young for the senior citizen center."

Her situation is not rare. Thousands of "unmarried" marrieds in the world are lonely in their couple lives. For reasons of their own, they choose to remain in a relationship that began with love but deteriorated through the years. Carin Rubinstein and Phillip Shaver, authors of *In Search of Intimacy*, found that one out of every four Americans suffers from loneliness and that 13 percent of married people say they are lonely and not in love. Their research also showed that men need women more than women need men because women are intimacy-givers while men tend to be intimacy-takers.[7]

Even within couples who develop friendship, life is not always smooth because one may not enjoy what the other enjoys. I worked with a couple who had very different social preferences. He hated parties and socializing, and she loved them. "At first I tried to change him," she admitted. "I'd drag him to a cocktail party where he'd head for a corner and stand there while I flitted around having a wonderful time. Then I'd be angry with him on the way home for being antisocial."

He nodded and said, "It was a no-win situation. I didn't want to go in the first place because I knew I would fail her and get scolded for it. We had an argument after every party. What she didn't know was how I envied her ability to talk with strangers and have a good time. I'm not good at that but I wish I was."

How did they deal with the stress affecting their relationship? He gathered the courage to tell her his real feelings—not that he disliked parties but that he was intimidated by them. A basic shyness, which she perceived as antisocial behavior, underlay his reluctance to attend that particular kind of social function. Once he risked his vulnerability to tell her he felt insecure in chatting with strangers, she reacted differently to his social needs.

"I felt awful," she said. "I didn't know he was shy and intimidated because he isn't that way with me or with our close friends."

Hers is a common attitudinal change that takes place in healthy couples once they dare to risk sharing feelings. He risked, and she followed through with an important response to that risk: She accepted his feelings rather than discounting them by reacting with, "Nonsense. What's there to be shy about? Nobody's going to hurt you. Just get out there and start talking."

A negative reaction thwarts a spouse's temptation to risk again. It says, "You don't have a right to your feelings." We see this constantly in couple interaction. He tells her she shouldn't feel angry or lonely or insecure on the job. She tells him he doesn't feel scared or depressed or inadequate.

Spouses do this because they don't want their partner to be himself or herself. Instead of respecting a partner's deep feelings, some spouses discount them, often with a motivation that springs from love. A wife may discount her husband's fear or inadequacy on the job because she sees him as the competent person he is and thinks that if she minimizes his feelings of inadequacy, he will no longer harbor them.

"I can't tell my wife any problem without having her offer a solution," one husband complained. "It drives me crazy. I don't want her solutions—I just want her to know about the problem."

We behave similarly with teenagers, and it drives *them* crazy, too. When they share with us that they're fat or ugly, we tell them they're not. Then we wonder why they become angry with such a loving response. If they feel fat and ugly, our words inflame them because we're actually telling them their feelings are worthless. (Besides, they expect parents to say such things. Didn't we tell them their kindergarten artwork was beautiful?)

A more effective response would be, "I know how you feel . . . I feel that way at times, too," or, "I'm sorry you feel ugly because I see such a lovely person in front of me." This doesn't discount their feelings but lets us share ours in a reassuring and supportive way.

An anonymous poem on this subject appeared in the book *Care of the Mentally Ill* which I will quote in part:

LISTEN

When I ask you to listen to me
 and you start giving advice
 you have not done what I asked.

When I ask you to listen to me
 and you begin to tell me why I shouldn't feel that way
 you are trampling on my feelings.

When I ask you to listen to me
 and you feel you have to do something to solve my problem,
 you have failed me, strange as that may seem.

Listen! All I asked, was that you listen.
 Not talk or do—just hear me.
Advice is cheap: 10 cents will get you both Dear
 Abby and Billy Graham in the same newspaper.
And I can do for myself; I'm not helpless.
 Maybe discouraged and faltering, but not helpless.[8]

How did the couple with the party stress respond ultimately to their diverse social needs? Once the wife realized the basis for her husband's dislike of cocktail parties, she didn't insist they attend as many, and she no longer left him alone in a corner but led him into conversations. She also no longer criticized him for his antisocial behavior. They gravitated toward smaller functions, inviting close friends with whom he was comfortable.

In talking about it, they indicated they both tried harder to collaborate, he attempting to join in more and she expecting less. They dealt with the actual stress—his shyness—to change the perceived stress—parties. In order to do this, they had to risk sharing some deep feelings of insecurity and compassion.

Nowhere does protection of feelings show up more than in a couple's sex life. In *Why Can't Men Open Up?* Steven Naifeh and Gregory White Smith tell of their first insight into this relationship: "Why can't men open up? That question, bursting with frustration and exasperation, was first thrown at us during a women's discussion group meeting we attended as part of the research for a book on sexual relationships. Expecting to catch some choice inside tips on how women like to have men make love, we found instead that making love was not really on their minds . . . "Jennifer, who hosted the meeting, told us, 'Speaking for myself, when things are going well in my relationship with my husband, the sex is good. When they're not, the sex is awful. It's as simple as that.' The other women nodded and murmured in agreement. Then she said, 'The relationship is everything. My husband doesn't need a book on how to make love. He needs a book on how to make a relationship. How to say "I love you," how to open up and let me into his life.' There was a commotion of agreement."[9]

3. The healthy couple develops conflict-resolution skills and creative coping skills.

Quite simply, the couples best able to deal with everyday stresses are those who develop workable ways of solving their disagreements and a fat supply of coping skills. Resolving conflict and coping are related, but not identical, skills.

Conflict-resolution skills depend largely on communication, while *coping skills* depend upon creativity, ingenuity, and perseverance. Some couples can have one set of skills and not the other. I met a couple who had excellent conflict-resolution skills. They could talk anything to death, share feelings, and emerge feeling good about themselves, but their family life was chaotic because they never *did* anything about the stresses attacking them. They just talked about them. The stresses went on and multiplied, and the couple finally sought help.

On the other hand, there are families in which stresses are addressed but not the conflict their resolution engenders.

Maybe insufficient money stress is resolved by a husband's taking a second job, but the resentment this instills in him can be explosive. Such couples are constantly putting out brush fires as a response to stress rather than dealing with the dry prairie.

Let's look at *conflict resolution* first. Philip Blumstein and Pepper Schwartz, authors of *American Couples: Money, Work, Sex,* an exhaustive study on how couples interact, explained their purpose in studying how American couples deal with stresses: "Today's marriages require a new level of awareness and more commitment to problem solving. When marriage was forever, issues could be left alone because there was the understanding that the couple had a lifetime together to work them out. Because this is no longer the case, we hope that a little information can help people to spot vulnerabilities and give their marriage the best chance it has to be a satisfying lifetime experience."[10]

All stressors do not lead to conflict, but many do, particularly those that have to do with money, sex, children, and shared responsibility in the family. When these reach a high stress level, they can damage the spousal relationship if the couple lacks the skills needed to resolve conflict.

Author and communications scholar Flora Davis says, "Almost all married people fight, although many are ashamed to admit it. Actually, a marriage in which no quarreling at all takes place may well be one that is dead or dying from emotional undernourishment. If you care, you probably fight."

Fighting is not the concern. The ability to resolve the fight or the conflict is the crucial determinant of a couple's success in handling the stresses that disagreement can bring into the family. A couple who deals with marital disagreement by going into a two-week period of silence is not dealing with the stress, and family tension will increase. A couple who shoves each other around or verbally abuses one another is increasing the stress level. The couples who cope with stress are those who resolve conflict—as simple as that.

And single parents, too, suffer increased stress if they are in continual conflict with former spouses. Robert E. Emery reviewed research findings that suggest that children's behavior may be affected more by the level of "family turmoil" surrounding the divorce than the separation itself; that many of the problems evident in the children of divorced parents were present long before the divorce occurred; and most significant, *that children of divorced parents whose family members are not in conflict exhibit fewer problems than those from two-parent families in which discord does exist.* From his evidence, the author suggests that parents try to keep children out of their conflicts and do everything they can to keep their individual relationships with their children supportive ones.[11]

Osolina Ricci, family therapist and author, says that divorced parents should get away from the idea that only mothers are important. "The parent who ends up with the least amount of time with the child is just as important to the child as the parent with the most amount of time," she says. "The good divorce is not a mystery, even though there are a lot of hard feelings . . . It's hard work to have a good divorce, but the amount of time the parents spend to make it a good divorce the first couple years will come back to reward them one hundred-fold three and four years down the line."[12]

In the Thomas-Kilmann Conflict Mode Instrument, the authors present five ways people usually react to conflict: avoiding, competing, accommodating, compromising, and collaborating. I quote here from an article, "When Couples Disagree," by Kristine Miller Tomasik in which she discusses these five responses to conflict.

Avoidance: "Avoidance involves sidestepping or clouding an issue, postponing or delaying, or completely withdrawing from the conflict. The avoider tends to say things like, 'Can we talk about this later?' or 'I hate to argue,'" according to Tomasik.[13]

I witnessed very little avoidance among couples who control stress well. One of their most noticeable features, on the contrary, is their early acknowledgment of a stress and their ability to recognize the actual, rather than the perceived, stress. They don't play word games or pretend a given stress doesn't exist. They open up the subject with words such as, "I don't like what's going on here" and "There's something we need to talk about." And they do. One woman married to a reformed avoider told about following him into the bathroom, locking the door, and saying, "We're not leaving this room until we talk about this and come up with some answers."

Competition: "Competition involves a power-play and an 'I win, you lose' stance," according to Tomasik. "The person pursues his own wishes at the expense of the other person. He tries to force his will on the other. The competitor may simply see himself as standing up for his rights, or defending the logic of a position."[14]

Again, competition as weapon is minimal among stress-effective couples, although many indicated that they had begun their marriage by competing and soon recognized the cost of it in resolving conflicts. "I found I lost even when I won," a husband said reflectively. His wife explained that at one time he would "bring in research to make points, figuring that once he made his case, I would understand and give in. It was maddening and one day I told him I wasn't his student or his employee but his wife." Gradually they turned to other ways of resolving conflicts.

In *Why Can't Men Open Up?* the authors speak to this competition, which seems to be particularly attractive to men. "When a man gets into the habit of hiding his emotions behind a facade of facts, he runs the risk of developing an exaggerated and unjustified reliance on facts, even in situations where feelings are more important. In fact, a man will often grow more coldly rational and concentrate more single-mindedly on facts, the more his emotions are in turmoil."

They continue, "Facts, of course, have their place in solving emotional problems, but by overemphasizing their importance, men avoid coming to grips with the ultimate reality of emotional disputes: feelings. Said one woman, 'He tries to make me feel foolish because I can't sit and calmly discuss our problems like two lawyers. But he's the one who's foolish. Who can sit and talk rationally when the most important relationship in your life is on the line? I think a lot of men use that as a defense mechanism.'"[15]

I found that the competition level exists strongly in marriages in which there's an imbalance of power. Whoever is the dominant partner has to win to preserve his or her power base (the dominant spouse is by no means always male), and the permissive one struggles to be heard. In some cases, the competition becomes covert instead of overt. A wife who loses on a childrearing decision buys something they can't afford as her way of "winning," although it has nothing to do with the initial conflict.

Like children who work out unique ways of getting even, spouses who constantly lose out in the distribution of power find ways of getting even. Rarely do healthy communicating spouses exhibit a boss-employee relationship. Self-esteem is usually equal in good relationships, and neither partner allows himself or herself to be pushed around by the other. *Accommodation:* "The accommodator sacrifices her own concerns to satisfy the concerns of another person," according to Tomasik. "She is operating from a 'You win, I lose' stance. She is often motivated by fear of hurting the other person's feelings, a wish to smooth things over, and a strong need to make the other person happy—even at her own expense."[6]

One wife, who tended to slip into accommodation to avoid conflict, deeply wanted to visit her mother, who lived several states away. She knew they couldn't afford airfare, however, so she didn't say anything about her wishes. One day her husband surprised her with a plane ticket, but she became conflicted. She wanted to go, but she worried that he really didn't want to spend the money, so she refused the ticket. He was hurt, so to accommodate him, she then accepted the ticket. This infuriated him, and he shouted at her, "Why do you always do things to please me? Stop trying to read feelings I don't have. Why don't you grow up and say what you want to say instead of what you think I want to hear?"

Now she was truly baffled. She was doing everything she could to please him and had only succeeded in displeasing him further. This, of course, is the cost of accommodation as a conflict response. When one constantly adapts to another's moods and desires, this usually results in submerged feelings in the accommodator that explode in other ways.

Compromise: Each person gives up something in order to resolve the conflict. Couples use compromise to deal effectively with temporary stresses, like both wanting to spend Christmas with their own parents. They may agree to spend Christmas Eve at one home and Christmas Day at another or this Christmas with his parents and next Christmas with hers.

Tomasik calls compromise a cheaper version of collaboration. It is useful on minor issues when couples need a quick decision and don't have time or energy to fully collaborate.[17]

Stress-effective families compromise constantly: If you take the car in to be repaired, I'll pick up groceries. I can type your paper for you if you get dinner, and so on. But compromise is not effective in situations which require permanent resolution because the underlying issues remain and will continue to emerge as conflicts.

Collaboration: "Collaboration," writes Tomasik, "with its concern for exploring all the issues and meeting everyone's needs, is best of all . . . How can husbands and wives learn to collaborate? If collaboration and negotiation mean trying to meet each partner's needs, then it's obvious that each person has to be sensitive to what the other needs, wants, and feels. But we are not mind-readers. The only way we can know for sure what someone else wants is if he tells us. And he can only tell us if he, himself, knows what he wants."[18]

So we're back to sharing open and honest feelings. Collaboration, commonly found in healthy spousal relationships, simply means looking at underlying issues and coming up with solutions that best meet mutual needs. If she wants to go to work and he wants her to stay home, this conflict may require more than compromise. Even though she might compromise by agreeing to work only part-time, both will be unhappy because she isn't at home when he wants her to be and she has to settle for a lower-prestige and poorer-paying job. The compromise didn't really satisfy either of them.

So how do they collaborate? First, by exposing why she wants to go to work. (Does she want some personal money? Does she feel foolish at parties when people ask her what she does? Is she looking for a way to escape volunteer work? Is she bored at home and beginning to dislike her home and family?) And then by exposing why he wants her to stay home. (Will her work damage his pride as breadwinner? Is he afraid she will take on more power in their relationship? Is he fearful she won't need him as much? Will she still serve him in the manner to which he has become accustomed? Will it mean he has to help more around the house and with the kids? Does he feel it's wrong for a mother to work outside the home?)

The reasons for a conflict here are multiple and may go beyond the physical issue of a wife's getting a job to deeper issues and feelings that must be surfaced to reach mutually satisfying solutions. Collaboration addresses the hidden issues behind the revealed one and points the way to satisfactory resolution.

If she wants to go to work because she feels unrecognized and undervalued as an at-home mother, the resolution may lie in developing areas that will give her this recognition: increased spousal support and affirmation, college, a volunteer effort or a cause. It doesn't have to be a job.

If he's resistant because he doesn't want to spend more time in active parenting, then he has to admit the issue is not her job but his reluctance to spend more time with the children. Why does he resist this? Does he hate to color and play catch? Is he doubtful about discipline? Has he turned these things over to her and feels threatened at the possibility of having to deal with them himself? If so, this is the issue that needs addressing before they can satisfactorily resolve the issue of her going to work.

Collaboration takes time and surfaces feelings, which is why many of us never reach this stage of conflict resolution. Yet, it is the skill most evident in stress-reduced relationships. It underlies a family's ability to deal effectively with other stresses addressed in this book: children, work, money, time.

I noticed that healthy single-parent families avoid conflict less and collaborate more when it arises. Why this is, I'm not sure, but where there is only one parent, she and the children seem more in touch with each other's feelings than where there are two parents. Perhaps because she is the only caregiving parent, she tries harder to hear what the children are really saying, and perhaps the children are more responsive to her feelings because no other adult is around to respond to them.

When a conflict erupts in the single-parent family, there's no opportunity for parent solidarity against the child or children, which alleviates children's frustration somewhat. The argument is fairer when it's one parent against one child rather than two parents against one child.

"We get our fights settled fast," a single mother told me, "because we have to live together and we're all we have. We try to come up with solutions that can satisfy all of us most of the time but if not, we give in at times."

Several single mothers pointed out the hazard of children going to their father for a different decision when they're unhappy with the one she's made. How do they handle this situation to reduce stress? Most said that if the issue was one that involved the father, like visiting rights or money expenditures, they permitted and even encouraged their children to get the father's opinion. "I'm happy to have him share some of the responsibility for these decisions," one single mother said.

But when the issue had to do with daily living in the home, such as chore allocation, bedtimes, and use of car, these mothers were united in their policy, reserving for themselves the role of sole decision-maker. "If I have to live with and be responsible for my children, then I have to retain the right to make those decisions," one explained. "I don't mind if my children complain to their father about my rules but I let them know that I consider myself the primary rule setter around here. I've found that if I let the children in on the negotation of rules, they don't feel the need as much to bring in their father."

Coping skills are discussed throughout this book so I will not develop them in depth here other than to say that the effective parents tend to collect, devise, and use a variety of coping skills rather than to depend upon the one or two most commonly used in our culture. For example, they don't automatically turn to grounding for every adolescent infraction but work out other consequences. When money gets tight, they don't automatically send a wife to work but try other methods of simplifying their life-style or share goods and services with others. Instead of automatically saying no to a child, they develop other responses. I loved the reaction of the mother whose eleven-year-old daughter wanted to use eye makeup. "You can use it as long as I can't see it," she said. It was a creative solution to a common family stressor.

Families who deal most effectively with stresses have hundreds of little solutions to share on allowances, television, sibling fighting, time pressures, and shared responsibility, and I will pass them on to you in the chapters ahead.

4. The healthy couple makes use of support people and systems.

"We couldn't have survived without our friends . . . "; "If I didn't have my family nearby . . . "; "The neighbors were there when we needed them . . . "; "I couldn't get over the support I got from our church . . . "

Stress-effective families and stressed families view support systems quite differently from one another. Stress-effective families see relatives, friends, groups, and community as valuable supports in dealing with stresses, while highly-stressed families view them as evidence of their own inability to deal with stresses. Culturally, we came to believe that a good family was one that could handle its own problems. If it had to call upon relatives or neighbors for help in other than an emergency, it was not quite as "good" as other families.

Whatever the origin of this myth, I am appalled to find it still operating within pockets of our culture. We find, for example, cases of child abuse in which parents refuse to ask for help because they see such a request as a sign of weakness. The supports are there for them—loving family, hot lines, church mothers-day-out programs, friendly neighbors, a good community social service system which offers preventive skills—but even so these parents will risk abusing their children when stresses get too high rather than admit they need support and help.

Clearly, the most stress-effective families make the most use of support systems. When they need sudden childcare or when there's an illness or a problem, they have people to call upon, people who will call upon them as freely in return. I know a single mother, never married, who has a ten-year-old daughter. When she decided to keep her baby, her disapproving parents told her not to come to them if she needed help.

"I tried to prove to them that I could do it alone," she told me, "and as a result I nearly collapsed in stress overload. My therapist suggested a support group of other single parents and it has been my salvation. We call each other when we need support. We sit each other's children, loan dishes, furniture, even money. But most of all, we're family to one another. They are far more family to me than my own family."

Her experience is echoed in many studies of family support systems, particularly one by Nancy Colletta (1981), who found that those parents with high levels of support were more affectionate toward, closer to, and more positive with their children, while those with low levels of support were more hostile to, indifferent toward, and rejecting of their children.[19]

In today's highly mobile and technological society, we're not likely to find our relatives and old friends nearby. They may be a thousand miles away and available as support in an emergency but not in an everyday stress situation.

But we find the structured support group stepping in to meet the need for close family and friend networking. In the past few years, I have worked with support groups for families of Vietnam veterans, parents of unwed teenage mothers, bereaved parents, single-parent and stepparent families, pregnant women, parents of chronically ill family members, parents of adolescents, and others. I have great respect for these groups and often encourage stressed couples to consider becoming part of a support group to give them affirmation and confidence in their parenting.

I believe that community and institutional leaders can better help families in stress. By serving as developers and coordinators of support groups when needs are perceived, leadership can truly lead families into systems that help them deal with and minimize stress in their lives. Support groups for the unemployed replace the need for cronies at the local bar in areas of high unemployment. Support groups for depressed housewives, for parents of new kindergartners, for families with chemically dependent adolescents, for parents with children out of control, for families on low budgets—all of these are valuable to families who don't have a natural support system nearby.

5. The healthy couple is adaptable.

Although many of these couples speak of entering marriage with set ideas of marriage and family life, they then mention —often with humor—how quickly they came to recognize and negotiate individual differences. Some spouses marry intending to change their partner to their own way of thinking.

Healthy couples adapt and borrow each other's techniques in resolving conflict and dealing with stress. One couple I interviewed spoke laughingly of their attitude toward sleeping late on Saturday morning. "When we married I was up at 6:00 A.M. to get at the housework," admitted the wife. "My husband slept until noon and I thought that was immoral. Now we both sleep until nine. We never made a conscious agreement about it—we just sort of evolved into it."

Whether or not to sleep late on Saturday is hardly a major point of stress, but the example does show how couples gradually come to respect each other's habits and needs. Adaptability is a feature found in stress-effective families.

When faced with a stress, adaptable couples are able to modify attitudes and habits to best meet it. An example of this ability may occur when a couple's employment conditions change. "When Peter lost his job, I was concerned, of course. But I knew we could scale down and get through it," reported one wife. "Our biggest problem was relatives who thought the world was going to end. We ended up reassuring them rather than the reverse."

Recently there has been intensive study on the family life cycle, particularly as it relates to stress and change. Dr.

Hamilton I. McCubbin and Dr. Charles R. Figley invited top family scholars to contribute their insights and research on families and the stresses families experience as they move along the life cycle from courtship to old age. These scholars came from many different perspectives. But, according to the authors, "In spite of these differences in perspective, it is remarkable how much similarity these scholars see in how families respond to different stressors. The methods of functional coping are very similar across the different transitions and demands. These coping strategies include seeking information and understanding of the stressor event; seeking social support from relatives, friends, neighbors, others in similar situations, and professionals; being flexible about family roles; taking an optimistic view of the situation; and improving family member communication."[20]

Because adaptability is fundamental to a couple's successful movement from one stage to the next in the family life cycle, it may be useful to sketch here the seven commonly acknowledged stages and show how couples negotiate shifts from one stage to the next with a minimum of stress.

THE FAMILY LIFE CYCLE— SEVEN STAGES OF GROWTH

Stage I: The courtship stage.
While this is the most fundamental stage, the one in which individuals choose to become a couple, it is also one of the shortest in duration. It begins at the point that the couple decides to make a relationship permanent and ends with the birth of the first child. At some point in this stage, the period of courtship and romance ends, and each individual falls out of love with the idealized partner and into love with the real one, warts and all.

It is also the point at which many individuals realize that a particular love affair will not make a good marriage and call off the relationship because it's not "going anywhere."

One of the secrets of a smooth and nonstressful transition into the marital stages has to do with the ability of individuals to give up the romantic stage for the deeper relationship involved in the next. Couples who marry before the romantic phase ends and the period of reality sets in have the highest divorce rate of all. "He isn't the man I married" and "She changed" are complaints we frequently hear from couples who marry after a brief courtship. Their expectations of ongoing romance are unmet, and they feel cheated when they discover the real mate.

Some couples find this situation painful, sometimes spending the rest of their lives trying to recapture the romance of the courtship instead of recognizing the deeper joys and rewards of whatever stage they are experiencing at the time. It's a little like the military family who always speaks longingly of its last base and never enjoys the present one.

The chief tasks confronting a couple in the courtship stage include developing a communication style, a social and spiritual dimension, an occupation, and a home together. It's at this stage that couples set habits of discussing or not discussing stressful areas like money, sex, work, and feelings, habits which will affect their ability to cope with stressors in their life ahead. "If only we could have started our marriage by talking about these things, we wouldn't be in the shape we are today," said one man who was speaking for many couples who defer open communication until a stress reaches problematic proportions.

Stage II: Birth of the first child.

The birth of the first child means more than just another person entering the couple relationship. Couples change significantly. Never again will they be as carefree as they were when they were simply two individuals married to one another. They are now father and mother, roles which for most couples never end.

Father means looking at work and life in an entirely different manner. Suddenly a young husband is aware of the immense responsibility he is handed in protecting this family and furnishing food, shelter, clothing, tuition, braces, camps, for the next eighteen years. He can no longer easily say, "Take this job and shove it," or, "Let's spend Christmas in Vail." Along with these new responsibilities come fears—fear of taking second place in his wife's affections, fear of the baby's fragility, fear of not being a good father, and a very realistic fear that the couple relationship will change.

Mother also means looking at life in a new way. Suddenly a woman becomes aware that she will never again be the carefree and independent person she was before having children. She finds herself on permanent call. Her dress and behavior become more conservative. She worries about children's illnesses and behaviors over which she has little control, and often feels as if she has failed when the children become sick or unruly. At a workshop last year, I asked participants to name the last time they were really silly. One woman said it had been ten years earlier. "Really?" I exclaimed. "What happened ten years ago that put a stop to occasional silliness?"

"My daughter was born," she replied, "and I didn't think mothers were supposed to be silly." Silliness is just one of the cultural taboos placed on young mothers.

Barbara Holland speaks to this transformation when she writes, "Maybe one of the reasons babies got so unpopular is that mothers get such bad press. Most young women expect to be wives someday, but who, these days, wants to be a 'mother'? It's like saying you want to be fat and provincial and fond of plastic flowers . . . Mothers have no status. Parturition wipes out brains, education, taste, and character. Your boss knows this. Your husband knows it. Even your children know it. All mothers are comic-strip people who must be outgrown and thrust away."[21]

A young mother's time becomes consumed by the new baby, and she feels guilty if her work outside the home or her housekeeping standards suffer. She's tired, feels less attractive, and wonders if her husband appreciates what she's trying to do.

"Having a baby can be overwhelmingly stressful to a marriage," writes Sue Miller in the *Baltimore Sun*. "It can leave the mother limp as a dishrag and with a minus zero libido. As the baby snuggles up to Mom and fills some of her needs, Dad can feel frustrated and abandoned. In some cases, the marriage can be placed in jeopardy, says Susan Fischman, who studied 194 couples to see what changes occur in sexuality and intimacy after a baby is born." Her conclusions? That having a child is a very stressful and crisis-oriented period of life which can be overwhelming unless the couple has lots of friends and support systems and looks for ways other than sex to preserve their intimacy.[22]

On a more personal level, author Maxine Hancock told about her married life right after bringing their first baby home. "Another point of conflict developed. Cam had been tender and considerate during my months of pregnancy. Now, suddenly, he was impatient and demanding. He wanted life to get back to normal—and soon. When, during the baby's second week, I rejected Cam's suggestion that we invite friends over for supper, his frustration boiled over into anger. 'Don't you think you're making just a bit much out of this whole thing?' he asked."[23]

The negative effect of this period is that marital satisfaction generally declines from the birth of the first baby until the leave-taking of the last from the nest, twenty-five or thirty years down the line. The positive is that couples who marry later and wait longer to have children have the lowest divorce rate of any group.

Couples who adapt effectively to this stage with the least amount of stress are those who most willingly give up the rewards of their earlier relationship—freedom, money, time — for the joys of creating a new being and watching their young child develop. Instead of focusing on their losses, they develop a newfound appreciation of one another as parent— "She's wonderful with the kids"; "He's such a good dad"— and they enjoy the simple pleasures of observing their children grow and of bonding as a family.

Even though studies show this stage as highly stressful, many couples report this period as the best in their marriage. They pay attention to their coupleness, and even though family demands are great, they tend to hang on to whatever it was that brought them together in the first place. They do not turn their lives over to their children exclusively but find time for themselves to talk, share, and enjoy one another.

I interviewed a young couple with three children who allocated two dollars a day for a neighborhood baby-sitter who came in and did dishes and watched the children while the parents took an after-dinner walk during the week. "We had budgeted ten dollars a week for entertainment," he said, "but by the time Saturday night came around, we realized we hadn't really talked since the week before and decided to spend it this way instead of on a once-a-week movie." What did they talk about on their daily walk? "Oh, big things," she laughed, "like what Timmy did to the cat and how bad the traffic was on Broadway."

What a wise young couple. They recognized that a relationship can't be deferred without damaging it. One of the stresses, in fact, reported by couples separated by distance during the week is the lack of sharing day-to-day details. By the time they reunite, the little items that make up the fabric of their days seem unimportant or are forgotten, and they feel a real sense of loss.

The major tasks of a couple in this stage generally surround childrearing: parenting and disciplinary styles, sufficient time and money for children, balancing work and family expectations, and communicating as a family. An auxiliary task, as mentioned, is that of keeping the couple relationship healthy and exciting. It's at this point that many couples begin to take separate paths that lead to loneliness later on in marriage. He is so consumed with work pressures and she with family needs that they put their couple relationship on a back burner, where it eventually becomes lukewarm or cold. Then when they try to recapture their intimacy years later, they are different persons and must begin anew. Frequently by the time they realize what they have lost, the relationship is beyond recapturing.

Stage III: Last child enters school.
Sociologically, this is a relatively new stage in family life. At one time, it was the stage in which the mother, freed from constant caregiving, became involved in volunteer work,

socializing, or hobbies. Today, it is more often the signal for women to reenter the work world, return to college, or get training for future careers. Because this phenomenon is relatively new, we haven't developed sufficient support structures, like adequate child care and shared responsibility in the home, to deal with the stresses this stage can bring to a family.

Again, it's more than a mere matter of an additional job. Outside employment changes mom, which in turn changes dad and the children. If the couple refuses to give up the expectations they had in the earlier stage— mother's availability, immaculate housekeeping, gourmet meals—the stresses can be enormous. Couples who adapt well are those who welcome a mother's increased self-worth and who encourage shared responsibility on the part of the husband and children.

"I find my wife much more interesting to talk to now that she has a job," reported one husband. "It isn't that she was boring before but she brings home ideas from work that are new to me and we both enjoy that. Also, I don't have to be her pipeline to the outside world anymore and that's tremendously frecing."

Common couple stresses at this stage include diminished housekeeping standards; guilt for not spending more time with the children; jealousy of a wife's work enthusiasm, job success, and male co-workers; insufficient couple time; and resentment over having to share chores. Couples who handle these effectively are those who talk about them and support each other. Generally, they develop new patterns of prioritizing time and sharing family responsibilities. Trust is the best thing a couple has going for them in this stage, an unspoken trust that says the other is acting in a way that is best for me because he or she loves me.

A wife's paycheck sometimes alleviates the financial stress which is high in many families, so the stress brought about by her absence from the home for forty or more hours is considered a trade-off. "When mom goes to work, the whole family goes to work," a marriage counselor told me, and he's right on target as far as healthy families go.

Stage IV: Adolescence.

Somewhere in the middle of Stage III, the oldest child becomes an adolescent, and this is a potentially stressful time for a couple who focuses backward instead of forward. It means giving up the rewards of compliant children, relatively smooth family interrelationships, youthful parenthood, and total authority, and instead recognizing the emergence of young adults who can drive and generally care for themselves, and looking forward to a time when they will leave home.

Although many couples dread their child's coming adolescence, it actually signals approaching freedom for themselves as well as their children. A comedian surfaced the feelings of a lot of parents when he said, "Life doesn't begin at forty. It begins when the dog dies and the children leave home." Studies indicate that he is correct. Marital satisfaction takes a great leap forward when couples who have kept their relationship in order find themselves child-free again. But to reach that stage, they have to experience adolescence.

A common couple stress during adolescence has to do with what's going on within the couple at the time. If they're having difficulty coming to terms with mid-life dreams and roles, they frequently use the adolescent as a scapegoat. McCubbin and Figley say that when parents feel productive, centered, and in control of their lives, relationships between them and their adolescent are smoother, but that adolescence can disrupt the adult's self-perception and sense of well-being.

"The presence in the home of an adolescent who questions parental values and customs may exacerbate the parents' own inner turmoil," they write. "The adolescent unwittingly contributes to the parents' developmental crisis in other ways as well. Parents in mid-life often become aware of the child's budding sexual attractiveness and vigor at a time when they perceive their own sexual attractiveness to be waning."

And that's not all. "Career reassessments can lead to the realization that one's own career has reached a climax. The dream of becoming a great writer, a college president, or a foreman conflicts with the reality that one falls short of the mark set in younger days. A father may feel resentment toward a son who is 'just starting' and for whom dreams and ideals remain possibilities.

"A mother may be resuming a career of her own or seeking ways of starting a career and may envy her daughter's opportunity to start early in life. As parents are coming to terms with sorting out their mistakes and the realities of their lives, adolescents have the hopes, dreams, imagination, opportunity, idealistic goals. The parent may feel envy and resentment; the adolescent may become impatient with limitations imposed by society and 'conservative' parents. Thus, two generational transitions exist together—often feeding on each other—with the potential for at least a mild amount of stress."[24]

Couples who adapt well tend to welcome adolescence rather than to dread it and attempt to hold it back. They sense its temporary nature and enjoy the development of their budding young adults. They expect stresses and work together on solutions rather than trying to eliminate the stress itself. "When our son began playing loud rock music, my first thought was, 'Thank God, he's normal,'" said a mother. "But it soon became unbearable and together we set some rules on volume, nighttime playing, and so on. He didn't always like the rules and did some testing, but then we didn't always like the music, either. We worked at it until we could all live with it fairly happily."

I will be dealing with adolescent behaviors and parenting in the chapter on children, but in this discussion of family lifestyle, I want to emphasize that emerging adolescents can change adults as well as harmonious family life. Healthy couples tend to recognize the difference between their own stresses and the stresses which arise when a child moves into adolescence. I found few who blamed one another for adolescent behavior, for example, a common practice in dysfunctional families.

The chief task at this time is to begin to negotiate with children as emerging adults while retaining a healthy couple and family relationship. At times this is very difficult and tests the fabric of the strongest family. Humor is a valuable gift at this stage if it's used positively.

Stage V: Launching.

This is the period in which young adults begin bouncing in and out of the nest. They're off to college but back home for summers or off to a job only to return when the job disappears and they are hungry. It can be a trying time for couples because it's so transitory. Just when parents get used to privacy and quiet, noise and activity reappear in the form of young loved ones who still need emotional and financial support.

But it's a terribly critical time in the development of both young people and their parents. The young are beginning to learn to survive without the family, and so are the parents. In his definitive work on healthy families, Dr. Jerry M. Lewis claims that there are two purposes to family life: to rear children who will leave and to retain the sanity of the parents. This stage is the testing ground for both.

Adapting couples realize conclusively that they will soon be alone again as a couple and that they will be a couple unlike the one they were before they had children. It's at this stage that they begin to renegotiate and revitalize a relationship that will be of much longer duration than the one they shared between courtship and the birth of their first child.

If they have allowed their relationship to center on children, they are spurred to find new mutual interests which will sustain them later on. I was intrigued by the many ways couples achieve this: through a political cause, a part-time shared career which may become full-time upon retirement, voluntary work, a sports interest which they didn't have time to develop in the childrearing years, an interest in computers, and, of course, college courses. One couple I met were taking a community college course on building a home in anticipation of building a modest cabin together someday.

All of these evidence coping skills noted earlier by scholars who study families and stress, especially taking an optimistic view of the situation and improving communication. When a couple takes a course on building a cabin together, it indicates optimism for the future and a willingness to work and communicate together in achieving a dream.

Stress in this stage chiefly affects parents who are unwilling to let their children go. They fear being together because they have little to share and lots of time to share it. So they look backward and tighten the strings to their children rather than look forward and loosen them. Their sanity has rested in their role as parents rather than as a couple, and it is now severely tested. "I won't even think of when the children leave," a mother wrote. "It will come soon enough and I will deal with it then." Couples who move smoothly to the next stage don't wait until the nest is empty to deal with potential loneliness and lack of relationship. They deal with it in advance.

The chief tasks of parents in the launching stage are to renegotiate and revitalize their relationship and to let the children go emotionally as well as physically.

Stage VI: Empty nest.

The children are gone. Retirement is coming. Healthy couples welcome both because they have prepared for this stage. They don't look back at what they have lost but tend to look ahead at being together, doing some of the things they have deferred, and enjoying their grown-up children. A chief task at this stage is the renegotiation of grown children as friends rather than as offspring. "I never realized how pleasurable this time of life could be," a successful father said. "I can listen to my sons talk about their lives and their work and not feel I have to give advice. It's great having children but even greater having them as adult friends." Smart father, lucky sons.

Empty-nest stresses most often mentioned include nothing to talk about, worries about grown children's marriages and grandchildren, health and money fears, too much together time, dissimilar interests, and loss of self-worth because of retirement.

With the existence of these stresses, why is it that some couples find this an exciting time? The answer lies in the preparation they have made for it, their flexibility, their optimism, and their ability to seek support from friends and relatives, especially those who have already experienced the empty nest. I can't emphasize enough the relationship between Stage V and Stage VI. Adapting couples don't suddenly find themselves without jobs and children but expect and offset these predictable stresses earlier in their couple life by preparing for life alone again.

Stage VII: Fulfillment.
This is the final stage, one that presumes declining health and eventual death. Of significance to younger couples who are apt to be the readers of this book is that the rewards of this stage are largely dependent upon earlier stages. If the elderly couple looks back upon life and family as worthwhile and meaningful, they live this stage in content and with optimism. They have, after all, a legacy to point to with pride—satisfying relationships with one another and with grown children. Past work success seems less important, which is one reason we hear these couples say, "Don't work so hard. Spend more time with each other and the children." They glimpse time expenditure in perspective because they have lived it.

Conversely, it can be a bitter time for couples if they feel they have failed as parents. I interviewed a seventy-eight-year-old grandmother who was exceedingly resentful. She recounted ungrateful children, a complaining spouse, and declining mobility as "rewards" for a life of sacrifice and hard work. I discovered that she never really developed a spousal relationship beyond that of parenting and as a result refused to allow her middle-aged children to grow away from her emotionally. She pulled every guilt string she could, which only caused her children to pull further away.

I use her here as an example of deferred life. She deferred her spousal relationship to a parenting relationship, her personal life to family life, and her rewards to old age. When she reached old age and found she could defer no longer, she realized how little of life's pleasures she had enjoyed.

Each stage of family life brings its own stresses and joys, a fact healthy couples seem to recognize. In presenting workshops on the family life cycle, I encounter certain predictable questions, the most common being, "What if you're living in several stages at once?" Most families are, but stresses are apt to stem from the most recent and least experienced stage. If a woman is pregnant but has a thirteen-year-old son, she is apt to experience the stress of adolescence more than the stress of beginning a family because she has already experienced the new baby stage and dealt with those stresses.

Divorced parents frequently ask if the stages fit their family structure, and the answer is yes, with some understandable qualifications. But even more than intact couples, divorced parents must be willing to let go of past stage rewards. If they focus on what used to be, they are deferring what is and the inherent rewards of the present stage. It may be tempting to relive past holiday memories, for example, but the stress-effective parent focuses on the present holiday, even if it means Christmas Eve with one family and Christmas Day with another. The outstanding feature of healthy parents, be they single or coupled, is that they look forward rather than backward.

In this chapter I have attempted to show that each family strength builds upon another. The expectation of stress and preparation for it at various stages requires communication which results in effective conflict resolution and leads to adaptability. This process is nurtured by social support systems like friends, neighbors, families, and groups. Where these strengths are present, the spousal relationship is strong and capable of dealing with predictable family stresses.

In summary, the stress-effective family
1. views stress as a normal part of family life,
2. shares feelings as well as words,
3. develops conflict-resolution and creative coping skills,
4. makes use of support people and systems,
5. is adaptable.

4

Money, Money, Money

Finances were chosen as a top stress by 58 percent of married men, 66 percent of married women, and 87 percent of single mothers.

* * *

"Money, money, money. The top ten stresses in our family all have to do with money. Money may not be the root of all evil, but it sure is the root of all stress."
                                        —Thirty-seven-year-old husband

The husband who wrote this in large print across the face of my stress survey may have been exaggerating, but he seconded the bulk of my respondents who named finances/ economics/budgeting as the number one stress in family life today. When I began researching why money is such a debilitating stress, I presumed that *insufficient money* would be the cause, but I was wrong. While families often name lack of money as the culprit and assume that if they just had more, their financial pressures would go away, my research reveals that those in all income categories named money as a top stress—those with incomes over $40,000 as well as those with incomes under $10,000.

So just having more money is clearly not going to make financial stresses in the family go away. How money is to be spent, who has spending power, when to take out loans, how to invest, how to deal with children's demands, and fears about future security are just a few dimensions of financial stress in modern families.

Blumstein and Schwartz, in their exhaustive study of American couples, state emphatically from their research, "*Couples who fight about money argue more often about how it is to be spent than about how much they have. Our data shows that couples argue more about how money is managed than about how much they have*—and this holds true despite their actual income level. . . . Conflict can occur when partners have different views about how the money ought to be spent, or when they disagree on the process to be used in making a decision. One partner may want all decisions to be fully discussed and jointly reached while the other may feel it is his or her right to make a spending decision without allowing any consultation. So, no matter how high a couple's income, there are still daily decisions to be made about spending it, leaving them much room for disagreement."[1]

The depressing paradox on money stress is that solving one pressure often gives rise to a new one. A family who overcomes insufficient income by adding another paycheck adds a whole new line of stresses like insufficient time, inadequate child care, and guilt. Couples who resolve conflicting how-to-spend issues may set themselves up for loan-payment stresses. Devising and keeping to a budget has strained many marriages.

So crucial is money to marriage that newly divorced Nat B. Read wrote a poignant article detailing the rise and decline of his marriage through checkbook stubs. "Like the grandfather clock that stopped, short, never to go again, our checking account measured our marriage from a time shortly after we were wed until it stopped, short, at check 3854, as dead as the marriage it had financed. Checking account 0255-04533 had measured our partnership, check by numbered check, in better times and worse, in sickness and in health, until we no longer loved or cherished, and in debt we did part. Check 1 launched the staggering debt of two young newlyweds hellbent to buy into the good life of mortgages, appliances, wheels, and gadgets. Twelve years and 3,854 payments later came the death knell: a check to General Telephone for $97.63

worth of desperate calls to counselors, lawyers, creditors, and friends trying to save or scuttle the marriage."[2]

There are probably other ways of measuring a marriage, but this checkbook journey graphically illustrates that marriage is still very much an economic union. Unlike other businesses, it gets tangled up in emotional assets like love.

Adult roommates who share a condominium don't share the same kinds of economic stressors that married couples do because they aren't committed to one another and to roles that say the person who makes the money has a greater say on how it is to be spent or that one person's security is the other's responsibility. Each roommate throws in a certain amount of rent and household money and assumes personal decision-making on how the rest of his or her money will be spent or saved.

Cohabiting couples tread the line between "just roommates" and married couples, embracing both legal independence and emotional attachment, but money can be a testing ground for this relationship, too. Blumstein and Schwartz found that in couples that are cohabiting, money is commonly kept separately. But if the couple marries, they take on the ground rules of marriage over time.

"The problem" said Schwartz, "is that couples don't talk about money before they're married. They don't view it as a policy, answering questions such as, 'What are each spouse's expectations?' or 'Who makes the decision on the important things?'"[3]

In their book, *American Couples: Money, Work, Sex,* they speak of money as the conversational taboo for couples dating today. "Money is often a more taboo topic of conversation than sex, and courting couples may discuss their prior sex lives while never raising the question of their economic histories. After all, it is not very romantic or interesting to talk about net worth or projections of income or one's indebtedness, so money becomes the last frontier of self-disclosure even though each partner may hold strong feelings about how money should be dealt with. Discussion of premarital sexuality has far outdistanced fiscal awareness."[4]

When I interviewed parents, I presented them with a list of money-related stresses and asked them to select the most stressful. I then asked them to respond to a number of questions about the role of money in their family life. Readers might find it useful to take a moment and reflect on which stresses they would name as most prominent and how they would respond to the questions. It is often revealing (and sometimes harrowing) for spouses to do this separately and then exchange responses.

FINANCES/MONEY/BUDGETING

Please check the most stressful areas you have experienced in dealing with finances, money, and budgeting in your family.

_____ keeping up with inflation
_____ agreement on scaling down expenses
_____ additional spouse going to work
_____ overtime work
_____ devising a budget
_____ keeping to budget
_____ balancing the checkbook
_____ need for savings
_____ children's allowances
_____ children's part-time jobs
_____ dual paychecks: who pays for what?
_____ fears about retirement funds
_____ investing: how/where?
_____ agreement on major expenditures
_____ agreement on everyday expenditures
_____ buying on time
_____ credit cards
_____ entertainment spending
_____ vacation spending
_____ college spending
_____ children's demands
_____ donations to charity/church
_____ in-law expectations
_____ taking out loans

_____ temporary unemployment
_____ permanent unemployment
_____ frivolous spending
_____ personal unaccounted-for monies
_____ other (please specify)

1. Do you feel you have satisfactorily resolved any of the above? If so, how?
2. How are you coping with inflation?
   _____ scaling down
   _____ overtime work
   _____ extra wage earner
   _____ substituting, exchanging, sharing goods and services instead of replacing them
3. Do you have a joint checking account? _____ Individual as well? _____ Credit cards? _____ Who balances the checking account? _____
4. How do you deal with children's needs for money?
5. Do you insist that your children save?
6. Do you expect your children to help with college monies?
7. Do you view money matters as a temporary or ongoing stress?
8. Do you discuss money problems and fears with your spouse?
   _____ About how often?
9. Do money matters put a strain on your marital relationship?
10. Does the major wage earner link earnings with self-esteem?
11. Does the nonworking spouse feel less valuable?
12. As a couple, what do you name as your greatest strength in managing your money?
13. Your greatest weakness?
14. Are you satisfied with your present life-style?
15. If you had a thousand-dollar windfall today, how would you like to spend it?
16. How are you likely to spend it?

How did healthy families respond? In order of priority, the most stressful areas included
—about retirement funds
—keeping up with inflation
—devising a budget
—agreement on scaling down expenses
—keeping to a budget
—need for savings
—credit cards
—college spending

Because we can learn much from what people did *not* choose, I think it's important that we look at these. *Rarely chosen* were
—children's allowances
—children's part-time jobs
—dual paychecks: who pays for what?
—agreement on everyday expenditures
—buying on time
—children's demands
—donations to charity/church
—in-law expectations
—taking out loans
—personal unaccounted-for monies

Stress-effective families also tended to cope with inflation by scaling down rather than adding extra jobs; to have a joint checking account rather than individual, with both balancing the account but not together; to have no set pattern on children's monies but a variety of patterns for different ages and circumstances; to expect children to help somewhat with college monies, usually in the area of personal expenditures and books; to view money as a temporary rather than ongoing stress; and, for the most part, to be satisfied with their present life-style.

Since these families represent all levels of income, the last two responses are worth our attention. I was intrigued to find that the same people who named concern for retirement security as their top money stress also claimed to view financial stress as temporary rather than ongoing and to be *relatively* satisfied with their present life-style. I asked many questions of these families, attempting to get at the root of this seeming contradiction. I discovered that the concern for retirement security is somewhat related to the length of time between the graduation from college of the last child and the retirement of the major wage earner but that the scaling-down ability of these couples has proved to them that they can survive. In other words, they fear retirement cutbacks in life-style, but they are prepared for them and they know they can live with them because they already have lived with cutbacks at some time or another in their marriage.

Discussing satisfaction with present life-style was more uncomfortable for these families. The answer I received most often was a slow "Somewhat." While this may seem inconclusive, highly stressed couples were rarely satisfied with their present life-style—whatever their income—and tended to allow it to affect their relationship. A noticeable advantage healthy families have going for them is the ability to enjoy family life and each other in spite of normal financial stresses. In contrast to others, these families tend to be more accepting of financial limitations and more hopeful that they will be temporary. They would prefer fewer financial stresses, but they don't defer present happiness in family life until those money pressures disappear.

Single mothers responded to the survey much differently than married couples did. Their most stressful areas included
—insufficient money to meet daily needs
—keeping to budget
—not receiving anticipated child-support monies
—keeping up with inflation
—taking out loans
—temporary unemployment

Clearly, a single mother's stress over money has to do with amount rather than use of money. Discretionary monies are so limited in these families that there are few arguments over how to spend nonsurvival funds. A good deal of stress occurs over whether or not monthly support payments will be met, even if the children's father has never missed a payment. One woman explained, "He has a good job, genuine concern for our children, and another family. But in today's economy, who knows when his job might get squeezed out? And if that happens, which of his families will come first?"

The great money stress experienced by single mothers gives rise to another stress if they try to alleviate money worries by taking a second job or working more hours. They feel guilty for spending more time away from children who have only one caregiving parent. "If I work more, I feel guilty," said one. "And if I don't work more, I feel guilty."

Many are forced to take out temporary loans and this adds to the stress level of the family. A broken arm, a malfunctioning car, an excessive heating bill—any of these can exceed the monthly income, and the single-parent family knows the fear of making loan payments on a survival income.

I was struck by how often single mothers mentioned money differences as a precipitating factor in their divorce. "We argued about whether the children needed shoes when we were married and we argue about the same thing now," one said ruefully. "He still claims I overspend, and I still claim he's unrealistic about today's costs." Then she added a reflection that I heard from several single mothers. "While there's less money to spend now, though, there are fewer hassles over how to spend it. It's freeing to be able to make a money decision and not have to defend it or tiptoe around."

I don't want to give the impression that healthy families have eliminated money problems and worries from their lives. On the contrary, they *do* find it difficult to talk about money at times; money can put a temporary strain on a couple's marital and sex relationship; and as in other families, the nonworking spouse tends to feel less valuable to the marriage and family. But these families exhibit certain characteristics that help them to deal more effectively with money stresses than do others.

—They talk about money.
—They do not link self-esteem with earning power.
—They develop money-management skills.
—They teach their children about money.

1. Healthy families talk about money.

While this statement may seem too simplistic, talking about money and what it represents in a relationship and arguing about expenditures are two entirely different things. As mentioned earlier, money is a taboo subject in many dating relationships and even in marriages. "We don't talk about money," one wife told me. "We fight about money." This family is far from rare.

Why is it so difficult for couples to share thoughts on the economic dimension of their marriage? Why are they reluctant to share feelings on what money means to them? Why are they afraid to discuss money? *Because money means power.* We hear this all the time, but how does that phrase translate into everyday family life? Here's one way: Our children understand that money means power when we tell them, "We get to decide which car to buy because it's our money." Or when we say, "Clean your room or no allowance." When we banned certain TV programs in our own family, we used the rationale that since we were the ones who were paying the cable bill, we had the right to decide what could be viewed.

Children have little power in the family because they are dependent upon us for goods and services—for survival. They have no income. That's why they want a part-time job as they get older. It gives them some independence. They can buy gas, which gives them some freedom. They can buy designer jeans rather than the familiar brands their parents stipulate. Emerging independence coincides with adolescent jobs and complete independence with self-support. When children no longer need their parents' support, they no longer have to do as their parents wish. And that's power, too.

The same power and independence struggle arises between spouses in marriage. According to the authors of *American Couples,* "In three out of four of the types of couples we studied we find that the amount of money a person earns—in comparison with a partner's income—establishes relative power. This seems a rather cynical finding, one that does not accord well with cherished American beliefs about fairness and how people acquire influence in romantic relation-ships. . . ." They quote a woman who said, "Gordon still has to have the last word on everything. We get annoyed with each other over that, but when I push back he reminds me just who supports me and the children. If I start to win an argument he gives me his big final line, which is something like, 'If you're so smart, why don't you earn more money? . . .'"[5]

When couples disagree over how money is to be spent, the hidden issue is who has the right to decide and why. And that's a power issue. It's why some couples don't talk about money—they don't want to address the risky issue of balance of power and self-esteem in their relationship.

They argue about expenditures, but they don't discuss money. Many wives do not know how much their husbands earn or what they have in savings. Paradoxically, these wives don't want to know because knowledge would mean sharing responsibility for family finances and future security. Just as children refuse to worry about the source of money but expect it to be there when they need it, these wives assign money worries to their husbands. By so doing, they buy into the dependency that leads to resentment. One married woman confided to me that she envied her career friends who never married, because her marriage was limiting and demeaning, and then she added, "But at least I don't have to worry about old age security and they do."

The struggle over money and dependency in the marital relationship has strong roots in tradition. Women have been acculturated to ask their husbands for money when they don't bring any income into the home. The resentment this engen-ders among women who work hard all day at home must be enormous.

My mother told me that when she was a child in the early 1900s, it was common for wives to present a grocery list to their husbands for their okay. These wives justified the need for five pounds of flour and a pound of butter, and their husbands doled out the exact amount to them before they went to the store. Many families had charge accounts at the corner grocery which husbands paid monthly, so these wives never even had cash in their hands. Men frequently went with their wives to choose a new dress or coat. These practices were accepted and unquestioned, just as we accept similar practices with our children. The wife was powerless, and the husband worried about the finances. A parent-child relationship.

This has changed dramatically, but ingrained money attitudes remain. Many women go to work because it's a sign of emergence and independence. When a modern husband says, "She's changed since she went to work," he's generally speaking of her new independence and self-assertion. She has more power when she has money of her own.

Another reason couples don't discuss money is because they don't want to surface painful value differences. Value differences appear in the marriages of healthy couples, but when they do, they surface early and are dealt with at the time, not shelved to emerge as financial issues later on. Interestingly, many healthy couples admitted to conflicting money attitudes when they married, but they overcame their differences through the influence of the other and the ability to resolve conflict—some of those resources that fatten the family account of stress-coping skills.

These couples talk more about money and argue less about expenditures. By discussing openly, they share fears, decisions, values, and budgeting. They reveal underlying attitudinal differences toward taking out loans, investing, credit cards, and children's allowances—sometimes heatedly but always openly. They recognize that occasional arguments about money may be inevitable but that talking and collaborating on decisions is preferable to allowing money pressures to accumulate and explode later on.

Marriage authority David R. Mace explains, "Once a couple have achieved the ability to share their hopes and fears openly, to assure each other of their mutual trust and caring, and to give each other understanding, support, and mutual affirmation, they should be able to manage their money without serious conflict. In every fight over family finance, the partners are in effect saying to each other, 'You don't understand and love me enough to see and hear where I am in this situation.'"[6]

After completing my questionnaire on finances, many couples noted their pleasure in discovering how many money problems they had overcome in their marriage. When I followed up with a question on how they overcame a specific issue, they inevitably replied that they *talked about it* and *talked about it* until they came to a mutually satisfying solution.

"When we got married, Joe was dead set against credit cards," said a wife. "He came from a family where credit was considered a weakness, almost immoral. But I had used credit cards before marriage and found them convenient. You can save money with them, too. If there's a sale and you don't have cash you can take advantage of savings. And you don't need to have so much cash around.

"We discussed it constantly and finally he agreed to get a credit card for one year. He found out that we could have one without misusing it. We're careful about paying off our monthly balance and have only once had to pay interest. And that was a godsend because we had to get a new car battery on vacation on Sunday. Try to find a place to cash a check then!"

As mentioned earlier, one of the family's greatest financial fears has to do with retirement and old-age security. The General Mills American Family Report of 1978-79, *Family Health in an Era of Stress,* states emphatically, "The high cost of food, the problems in meeting daily expenses and the worry about not being able to save for the future head the list of pressures on the American family. And mounting inflation has had both a direct and indirect impact on the quality of health care and health practices of the American family."[7]

When couples develop a practice of talking about money openly, they tend to foresee potential disagreements and stresses and deal with them before they erupt into full-blown arguments. Some couples do this on an ad hoc basis while others develop a routine. I found it common for the latter to discuss financial differences, expenditures, and dreams once a month when they went over the checking account and budget together. However they work it, couples who talk about money are better able to resolve money stresses.

Single-parent families tend to talk about money more than dual-parent families, probably because there is less of it and greater need of consultation and agreement on spending. Children in these families are often brought in on the decision-making and resultant fiscal responsibility. As I wrote at length in *Traits of a Healthy Family*, children in single-parent families tend to be more responsible generally in many areas of family life, but this responsibility is most evident in money matters. They seem to know and accept with relative equanimity the change in life-style a divorce brings. When they witness their mother attempting to fill both roles of wage earner and caregiver, they tend to demand less and complain less about lack of sufficient money.

Children in single-parent families can become very good at economizing and seeking out bargains. "I read all the grocery ads and clip coupons," an eleven-year-old submitted proudly. "When my mom comes home we all decide together how much we can spend and what to get for next week's suppers." The pride shining through his words revealed his sense of fiscal responsibility in a family that prior to the divorce never gave grocery bills a second thought.

2. Healthy families do not link self-esteem with earning power.

I found that these families put a much higher value on the homemaking and parenting skills of mothers than other families. They tend to affirm the mother and appreciate, rather than depreciate, her value at home. I found few husbands in this group who valued themselves over their wives simply because they earned a paycheck and their wives did not.

However, even among this group, I discovered that full-time at-home wives tend to devalue themselves somewhat because they are not bringing in a paycheck. Because we live in a society that honors people for what they do rather than who they are, we can easily see how women begin to devalue themselves if they have little earning power. I met a woman who went to work at a job she disliked and didn't need financially but who felt that social pressure demanded that she do something other than stay home once the children went to school. "I really enjoy homemaking," she said, "but when someone asks me at a party, 'What do you do?' and I say, 'I make meat loaf,' they find someone else to talk to fast."

Even though they may not want to hear about meat loaf, people would probably accord her more respect if they understood her inherent value.

Here is what the 1984 *American Almanac of Jobs and Salaries* has to say about the value of the adult American woman who works in the home. "According to divorce lawyer Michael Minton, the dollar figure value of a housewife's work is $40,823, to be precise. He breaks down the job into different categories and numbers of hours performed weekly and multiplies by the going rate. Some of the categories: food buyer, nurse, tutor, waitress, seamstress, laundress, chauffeur, gardener, nanny, cleaning woman, errand runner, interior decorator, bookkeeper-budget manager, child psychologist, and public relations woman-hostess.

"On a more official level, a 1977 study by the Department of Health, Education, and Welfare estimated that the Gross National Product would be 25 to 40 percent higher if household work were included as part of the national output."[8]

I found that in strong relationships, family members grant esteem to each other regardless of their earning power. In single-parent families, where the caregiving parent—usually the mother—must combine roles of breadwinner and sole nurturing parent, children become very good at affirming and sustaining their parent's self-worth, even though the income may be slight and the mother's nurturing time limited. "If it weren't for my kids' support, I think I'd give up," said a single mother whose time and money stresses were enormous. She speaks for many others like herself.

Likewise, husbands in strong relationships are not accorded esteem by the amount of money they bring in. Several of the couples I interviewed indicated that at times in their marriage they lived with unemployment or diminished salaries but that it did not affect the nature of the relationship. This attitude is very different from that of families who hold the wage earner in low esteem because of low wages or unemployment. A 1983 study on economic stress among farm couples found that the impact of economic distress on the marriage can be judged by the pattern of blaming. Couples who reported greater economic distress also reported that they blamed each other more for financial situations. The authors of the study concluded that economic distress and blaming correlated among couples.[9]

Unemployment is probably the best indicator of how strongly individuals link their self-worth with work. One teenager described his father's sudden loss of job. "It was like he wasn't a good person anymore, you know? But he was the same person he was the day before he got fired—he just felt like he flunked or something."

Unemployment stresses can be catastrophic for some families and strengthening for others, depending largely on how much the earners equate their self-worth with the job. If they are unable to separate the two, the family is likely to suffer from their sense of failure. On the other hand, strong families tend to rally and support one another when there is a loss of job status. They find ways of dealing with financial shortages without overtly blaming the unemployed wage earner. With unemployment as with other stress, the difference between healthy couples who seek solutions and unhealthy couples who seek a place to lay the blame is most evident.

3. Stress-effective families develop money-management skills.

Most couples enter marriage with minimal financial skills. They may know how to balance a checkbook and make payments on a car, but for the most part, young singles do not budget, own a home, or prepare for retirement. These come with "settling down," and emerge as issues as soon as the leftover wedding cake is eaten.

Healthy couples learn to control money stresses together. Rarely did I find the practice of turning financial matters and worries over to one partner among these couples.

Nor is money regarded as his or hers, but theirs. If there is sufficient income, healthy families often budget discretionary monies for each spouse and child, but generally speaking, they tend to pool their resources and draw from them for mutual expenditures. I found some stress-effective couples who develop an agreement on dual paychecks for convenience purposes: he pays the rent, utilities, and car expenses, while she pays for groceries and clothing. Others deposit both paychecks and draw from the account for household and recreation needs. Whichever they choose, they tend to be satisfied with the arrangement they have developed. "We should be satisfied," quipped one. "It took us eight years and a lot of arguments to reach this point."

Here are the four most common money-management techniques I noted among healthy families:

Budgeting: While families with the least money stress tend to budget, their budgeting techniques vary significantly. Some plan a careful budget at the beginning of each month and work to stay within it. They evaluate their efforts at the close of the month and keep a watchful eye on what they spend. As one who keeps a much looser budget, I was startled at how quickly these families could give me their average weekly expenses for food, gas, and so forth. One family even shared, without opening a notebook, their average weekly food costs in dollars *and cents.*

More of the families I studied tend toward a general budget. They plan for fixed monthly costs like home, car, and medical and insurance payments and then divide remaining · funds into savings, food, clothing, recreation, and miscellaneous. Most have some kind of savings plan, with several utilizing off-the-top payroll deduction programs. "If we don't see it, we don't spend it" is a familiar comment made by these families.

"What happens if your budget doesn't work?" I asked and again received replies as diverse as the families themelves.

"It never works," chuckled one husband. "We never stay within it but it's there as a goal and we come pretty close."

Another family disagreed with that thinking. "If you never stay within your budget, then you need a new budget. It's better to budget realistically and stay within it than draw up a fantasy budget and never keep to it." But both families were satisfied with the way their budgets worked.

Many couples who have developed relatively financially stress-free marriages have long-range untouchable savings for their children's education and their own retirement and some easy-to-get-at savings if there's an unbudgeted need. When they say they don't stay within the budget, they don't, but part of their budgeting procedure consists of putting a share of each paycheck into savings for breakdowns, repairs, and other budget busters. So, in a way, they are staying within the budget even when they are not.

This kind of budgeting is more fundamental to stress-free family life than it appears. A family financial consultant who works with families of bankruptcy reported that unexpected repairs, replacements, trips, and medical bills are inevitable and should be considered ordinary expenses. "We know things are going to break down and kids are going to fall down. It's a part of family life. Yet few families carry a contingency fund for these so-called emergencies and their budget collapses along with the washing machine. When families have a cushion, they don't fall apart when something out of the ordinary happens. In fact, I emphasize to my clients that the real test of an effective budget is this: can it absorb an unexpected unbudgeted repair without affecting the marriage or family?"

How do families learn to budget? By trial and error, by panic and prayer. I didn't find a single couple who had ever used a family financial consultant for help with monthly budgets and spending (as contrasted with a large number who had used an investment counselor at one time or another). When I asked them if they would consider professional help with the family budget if they felt they needed it, they were uncomfortable with the idea. Two single mothers had attended classes on budgeting as a part of a postdivorce workshop. Both commented that they wished they had learned budgeting skills much earlier in their lives.

Just as we find money hard to talk about between ourselves, we find it even more difficult to discuss with others, particularly those who might criticize our money handling. So we'll go to accountants for help with our income tax and personnel directors for information on company benefits, but we don't go for help in learning to set up and live within a reasonable budget.

I have noted this repeatedly in my work with military families. Because of their youth, income, and education level, enlisted personnel tend to use few money-management techniques. Their expenses frequently consume most of their paychecks on payday, and they are left with little for food and nothing for recreation the last couple of weeks of the pay period.

In order to offset this, bases offer free financial counseling to couples who can't seem to operate within the same salary as others in similar situations. But, according to military ombudspersons, few couples who need it actually take advantage of this free service. "They are ashamed of needing it," one Navy ombudswoman told me. "We make it as confidential and non-critical as possible but still they won't come. It's a stigma of sorts. We've found that couples will go to the chaplain for marriage counseling before they come to us, even though money is often the precipitating problem in their marriage."

She would likely agree with Blumstein and Schwartz that the subject of money is taboo among couples and particularly between a couple and an outside party. Even healthy couples do not like to talk about money issues with outsiders. Not only are couples reluctant to make use of trained family financial advisors—who, incidentally, are available free of charge at many banks—but they don't go to their informal support systems (friends, relatives, co-workers) for help with budgeting and financial matters, either. We may talk readily about problems and philosophies of marriage, health, and childrearing, but rarely do we talk about expenses, income, and savings.

With money named as the top stress in family and marital life, how can we allow ourselves and our young couples to enter marriage so ill-prepared in this area? And many couples remain uneducated in money matters. Blumstein and Schwartz found that 34 percent of married couples were still fighting over money management after a decade of marriage. Today's wives have learned more about nutrition than about money, even though few marriages are stressed by nutrition. Most spouses indicate they learned to handle money by themselves with a little help from magazine articles and informal conversations. However, their primary skills emerge from trial and error—and many couples never get beyond the trial-and-error stage. Couples frequently feel as if money manages them rather than the other way around.

If I may be forgiven a plea here, it is that we build into our other adult courses and workshops a dimension that will help couples begin to deal with money in a knowledgeable and skilled fashion. Church courses on marriage can include gritty marital issues on spending money as well as more esoteric issues like couple bondedness. Wellness centers and day-care centers can offer occasional sessions on financial wellness and developing responsible money attitudes in children. Schools, banks, community recreation groups, voluntary organizations, professional groups, fraternal organizations—all can build practical money-management education into their programming if they focus on needs in the family and their responsibility in meeting these needs.

Coping with inflation: One of the most frustrating and stressful areas of money in family life today has to do with inflation. Couples are running, not to get ahead as their parents did, but to stay even. They try to stay even through second jobs, dual paychecks, overtime, and children's work, all of which create enormous time stresses and pressures. Real income has fallen behind as costs skyrocket. Even the family who budgets carefully is tempted to throw up its hands in despair at the end of a month in which, despite strenuous work schedules, no money is left for fun or for the future.

A *U.S. News & World Report* article, "The Average American Family, Then and Now," points up the contrast between families of 1963 and 1983 in many areas of life. We have moved from 48 percent graduating from high school in 1963 to 71 percent in 1983 and from 11 percent graduating from college in 1963 to 20 percent in 1983. Likewise, 41 percent to 51 percent of our major household earners have moved from blue-collar to white-collar jobs in this twenty-year span.

Does that mean that life is better for the majority of these families who evidence higher education and job status? Not necessarily. Using 1983 dollars, the median family income between 1963 and 1973 grew dramatically from $20,000 to $29,000, but by 1983, inflation forced buying power down to an estimated $27,000. This points out that although income may be more, we're losing ground in what it will buy.

All of this has much to do with how we perceive and deal with stress in our lives. The report summarizes, "Buffeted by economic and social storms, families in the U.S. are changing in just about every conceivable way. A new look at shifts that have occurred in the past two decades shows, among other things, that families are becoming smaller, are moving south and west, have more of the good things of life but have failed to keep pace with inflation."[10]

One clear way families are trying to deal with inflation is by having later and fewer children. Not only is a small family less expensive to care for, but it also allows both parents more freedom to work. However, there's an emotional cost involved in this solution. Many couples feel they must choose between children and a comfortable life-style.

In a delightful article, "Babies Aren't As Cheap As Yachts But They're a Lot More Fun," author and mother Barbara Holland tells us, "It's sad that babies have gotten so expensive, and so serious. Financially, they've inched up into the same class as owning a yacht. The U.S. Department of Agriculture says you can raise a basic, no-frills child for $134,000, assuming it goes forth to earn its own living on its 18th birthday, which is quite an assumption these days. For those more ambitious, a college-educated son will cost, according to a new study, $226,000 and a daughter will cost $247,000.

Obviously, parenthood is a financial handicap of the first order, and a lot of people might opt for the yacht as a more entertaining way to blow a quarter of a million."[11]

The most revealing statistics linking family income with family stress, however, come from a 1984 Gallup Survey on hunger and deprivation in America contrasting 1984 with 1974. The question was asked, "How often do you worry that your family income will not be enough to meet your family's expenses and bills—all of the time, most of the time, some of the time, or almost never?"

NOT ENOUGH TO PAY BILLS

	1984 %	1974 %
All of the time	20	13
Most of the time	15	12
Some of the time	30	36
Almost never	34	38
No opinion	1	1
	100%	100%

Source: *PRRC Emerging Trends 6*, no. 3 (March 1984):5.

When we compare these two decades, we see the stark fact that in spite of real income increases, families today worry more about money than they did ten years ago, with 65 percent worrying about having enough to pay bills at least some of the time. Because many have grown accustomed to a life-style they can no longer support, they feel as if they have failed, and this is exceedingly stressful.

Our society expects each generation to experience a higher standard of living than the one before. When this expectation is not met, many cannot accept the fact without bitterness, particularly men who compare themselves with their fathers. These men are frustrated much of the time, and their frustration often emerges as anger toward the family for expecting and demanding too much. "I am working my buns off for this family," complained one husband, "and all they do is gripe because we don't have enough money for everything they want and because I'm not spending enough time with them. How can I, for God's sake? I'd like to throw it all in and run away to Hawaii."

In their definitive book on the subject, *Stress and the Family*, editors McCubbin and Figley write, "Although inflation is a historical, cyclical, economic phenomenon in America, it has only recently been examined by social scientists as a stressor or source of family stress. Virtually no one since the Great Depression has attempted to examine how and why some families are strengthened by severe economic conditions such as inflation, while others succumb to financial disaster."

They quote a 1979 study which found that "the more families felt they suffered from inflation, the more they reported that their marriages suffered. Furthermore, as the incidence of staying at home increased, due in part to cutbacks in family entertainment, reports of marital strain increased . . . [but] in some families economic pressures resulted in closer ties between spouses as they increased communication to cope with economic adversity. Parents reported that even children were more helpful and attempted to pitch in more frequently than when the family was not faced with economic hardship."

These authors hold that families can adapt by using any one, or a combination, of four managerial strategies to combat the effects of inflation upon family purchasing power: (1) *Increase income:* The most obvious way is also the most familiar—the wife goes to work to help increase monies; but other ways to increase income include working overtime, additional jobs, and work in the home, such as child care. (2) *Reduce expenses:* Most common reductions in order of priority are cutting down on food costs (buying less food and less expensive brands), entertainment, eating out, and clothing. "Despite rapidly rising fuel prices, families have been reluctant to cut back on transportation," according to the authors. (3) *Extend resources on hand:* According to McCubbin and Figley, this coping strategy may be one of the most realistic for a majority of American families. Reducing waste and repairing or redesigning rather than discarding, and increased reliance on friends for sharing or exchanging transportation, baby-sitting, clothes, and food are ways families extend resources. (4) *Substitute, exchange, or share goods:* This possible coping strategy presumes the family has goods, such as crafts, produce, services, or equipment, to share or trade with relatives and friends. Sharing baby furniture, children's clothing, and the like is a familiar pattern in many families.

Finally, McCubbin and Figley point out that the very process of trying to cope with inflation can create sufficient tension to make some families dysfunctional but that inflation itself is not the stress that causes family breakdown; rather, the breakdown occurs because the family does not understand what is happening or how it can get control of the situation.[12]

I found in my research that healthy families tend to scale down more effectively than others. *They do this by revising their expectations.* Although at one time they may have expected expensive annual vacations, for example, they accept that these are no longer achievable for them and settle for camping or day trips in their own states. Because they don't continue to expect financial improvement, they also don't suffer disappointment which would add to their stress level. When we expect less, we are disappointed less. Those who refuse to lower expectations also tend to depend more on credit, which adds to financial stress. "We'll worry about it when the bills come in" may offer temporary relief from financial stress but increases stress in the long term.

Families who deal well with inflationary pressures tend to scale down in all areas of life. They will add a bathroom rather than buy a bigger dream home. They eat out less and at less expensive restaurants. They shop less impulsively. They collaborate more on major purchases.

One family reported that ten years ago they automatically assumed they would turn in their car on a new one every three years, but now they are satisfied to keep their family car in good running order longer. "It's not really that important anymore to drive a new car," they said. "We've changed a lot in ourselves and our values as a result of inflation."

Stress-effective families also tend to exchange services as a way of coping with inflation, although not as commonly as they use scaling down. I found many cases of child-care cooperatives, trade-offs in transportation, and shared purchases with other family members and friends. Perhaps the most unique was offered by a couple who told me that they pool gardening, carpentry, automobile, and snow removal equipment and services with three neighbors. In the springtime, they explained, the neighbors bring all their gardening tools to the corner where their four backyards meet and leave them there for communal use. One neighbor roto-tills everyone's garden, while another sprays trees later on when the bugs get hungry.

Our own family exchanges in two ways. My husband, a fine amateur photographer, takes and develops the photos of a relative's family for their Christmas cards, and that relative does our income taxes. I present workshops at a beautiful retreat center in exchange for our family's use of a cottage on weekends. It's a good exchange for both of us. The center doesn't have to pay presenter fees, and we have our own family cabin without making payments. Nor do I have to claim any income from my work there.

Developing effective purchasing patterns: Families with good financial skills develop a pattern of decision-making on purchases that eliminates the need for stressful arguments each time a potential purchase comes up.

Couples I've worked with constantly emphasize the need for time and understanding in developing a collaborative attitude toward purchases. Many spoke of deep differences toward spending, credit, and the need for accumulation of goods when they were first married. Sometimes these attitudes came from their own parents' attitudes toward spending, but many couples developed spending and saving patterns that were effective for the single life but in need of revision for healthy financial relationships in a marriage.

I am struck by how commonly healthy couples distinguish between discussion of major versus everyday expenditures.

They tend to respect each other's everyday decisions on expenditures without needing to discuss them unless there's some unusual reason to do so, like reduced wages or high monthly bills. She doesn't question his spending on things like car or house repairs or fishing gear, and he doesn't question her spending on groceries or kids' clothing or needlework.

But when it comes to major purchases such as furniture, a new car, expensive clothing, trips, and the like, these couples develop a way of sharing their own feelings, fears, and attitudes that takes into consideration the other's possibly divergent attitudes and opens the way for collaboration. Hearing a couple talk about how they approach each other in matters of major spending reminds one of a complicated mating dance of exotic animals. "We always begin by saying, 'I want to talk about a silver toothpick,' one woman said, 'because that's what we called some of those awful useless wedding gifts we got.' And the other usually says, 'The toothpick is pretty short this month,' or, 'We're rolling in toothpicks this year,' and then we get on with the discussion of what we want to buy, why we need it, and so on. Lots of times we put the major item on a back burner, but that way, at least, we can plan for it a few months down the road."

Often when couples can't agree on a major purchase, one will give in but then ask for the right to make the next decision; or they compromise. "I really didn't want to buy cheap living room furniture," a wife shared, "but my husband didn't want to spend for quality furniture. We tried to convince each other but it was clear one of us was going to be very unhappy either way. So I asked him if it was agreeable to put the money for cheap furniture in the bank for a year and live with what we had and then next year buy a better quality. So that's what we did. I think he knew then how much I disliked the cheap furniture." Another couple with the same issue might have decided to buy just one piece a year or agreed to have the old recovered.

But sometimes issues on major spending just can't be mutually resolved to the satisfaction of both. If he wants a new car and she doesn't and both are really committed to their stand, the presence or absence of a new car in the driveway can cause all kinds of other tensions and stresses in their relationship.

How do healthy couples deal with seemingly unresolvable situations that present themselves to all marriages at times? I found that they tend to give in. If they have tried reasoning, compromise, and collaboration and can't make them work on a specific purchase, one will realize the issue means a great deal to the other and scrap his or her own feelings and desires *this time* because he or she cares for the other. When I asked couples about these spending standoffs, they had all experienced them and had all sacrificed their own wishes at times in their marriage, but they stressed the temporariness of giving in. "When I give in on something important, I expect her to give in next time it's that important to me," a husband said.

Most of these couples also indicated that they do not get pleasure out of a purchase if it makes the other unhappy. Whether the stress is a result of money, parenting style, or working hours, "winning" the argument is not satisfying to the healthy couple because they care about each other's feelings and they don't want to damage a caring relationship in order to get their own way.

Money is often withheld to show withholding of feelings. Financial writer Carol Colman says, "Money becomes an emotional currency. It's very hard for people to find a concrete expression for their emotions, and money is concrete." She interviewed a woman who ran up three hundred dollars monthly in long-distance phone bills after moving with her husband so he could take a better, but more time-consuming, job. She felt he was putting his career before their twenty-year marriage, and the bills were her way of forcing him into a confrontation about their problems. They ended up in counseling.[13]

Money is also used punitively by, for example, a spouse who buys an unaffordable item to get even with his or her partner for inattention or some spousal transgression.

And money can also be used to compensate for lack of time with a spouse or children. A husband may substitute an expensive gift or luxury item for attention to family. I found the stress-effective couple free of these money attitudes and games.

Planning for retirement and old-age security: Couples I interviewed cited preparation for this time of life as the most stressful. Even if they have developed good money-management skills and are able to live a satisfying life-style by cutting back to combat inflation, all worry about the future. They fear that if inflation continues to gallop at the speed it has for the past decade, then any savings they accumulate during the time of rearing a family (when they really need the money) will be worth a half or a quarter of what they are now. "We're working two jobs just to stay even," one couple reported. "How can we not worry about having enough money when we retire?"

They fear that Social Security and other benefits may not be around by the time they retire. They realize that old age is getting longer in duration and medical costs are becoming astronomical. Fear of poverty in later years hangs over their heads. I can't emphasize enough the permanently stressful fears with which adults of all ages live in respect to future security. Ironically, at this time of wealth and technological advancement in our society, we are living with possibly the least amount of security. Earlier generations have lived with immigrant poverty and great depressions, but those were accompanied by a cultural tradition in which the younger generation assumed responsibility for the welfare of their elderly parents, a tradition that has become obsolete and is even considered dishonorable by a great number of our elderly.

Stress from fears for the future filters down from parents to children and explains the fairly recent phenomenon of college graduates' intense interest in pension plans of potential workplaces. Unlike their parents, who expected to move from job to job in a promotionary fashion, or to try out a variety of companies before settling on one at age thirty or so, today's young people focus simultaneously on entering and retiring from the work world.

Families who deal well with other economic stresses tend to have some kind of savings and investment plan, but there's often friction between the spouses on present versus future spending. I found many couples in which one spouse, most typically the husband, wants to put more money away for the future while the other wants to spend more now. This is understandable, for traditionally we have assigned old-age security to the man of the family, and present life-style to the woman. Healthy couples tend to collaborate better on this, as on other money issues, than do couples in which the spending-saving conflict causes ongoing stress.

The single device mentioned most often by healthy couples in achieving savings is the payroll deduction savings plan. "When we had the money in hand, we were tempted to spend it," many reported. "But when it's taken out before we ever see the check, then we can't consider spending it except in an emergency." Stress-effective couples come to an agreement on how much they can save and try to do this off the top of monthly monies. By doing so, they don't have to argue the issue every month, a disagreement that can escalate to ongoing tension and recriminations about her spending too much and his not earning enough.

Several couples indicated that when an annual raise went into effect, they would add the raise to their deduction so that their savings increased. Doing this may mean, of course, more stress in trying to live within a budget that increasing costs can strain. And families may be trading the stress of retirement for the stress of trying to make ends meet today.

Single mothers, who made up the bulk of my respondents in the under $10,000-income category, have the least amount of old-age security and, paradoxically, the least stress over it. Single mothers existing on the poverty level find they are too busy focusing on surviving from day to day to be able to prepare for old age. From those I interviewed, I heard responses like "I'll have to worry about that later" and "Maybe my kids will have to take care of me." As I mentioned earlier, children in single-parent families tend to be less demanding and more responsible in conserving money.

They also tend more to expect to help their mothers financially later on than do children of dual-parent families. Because single parents worry less about the future than do couples, they did not name this as one of their top economic stresses. And because the children of single parents do not expect them to furnish college monies (there aren't any) and expect to get more loans and to work if they want college, single parents also do not worry as much about college monies.

Oddly enough, then, not having money can alleviate stress as well as cause it. We must not forget, though, the stress involved, particularly for single-parent families, in trying to live day to day on insufficient income. I admire greatly the mothers who achieve this without permitting ongoing economic pressures to affect their family relationships.

4. Stress-effective families teach children about money. Families vary significantly on how they foster children's attitudes about money and how to use it. The healthier the family, the more the parents recognize the need to devise policies on money that help children learn to use it wisely. Audrey Guthrie, a specialist in consumer education and family management at West Virginia University, says, "Many parents are concerned their children will reach adulthood and have few money-management skills. We teach children how to earn money, but not how to manage it."[14]

College counselors agree and tell us that lack of money-management skills is one key contributor to freshman maladjustment. One told me, "We get kids here who have never had to live within a personal budget before and they can't handle it. They have a new checking account and they think that the money in it will last forever. By the end of the first month they look at the balance and realize they've spent half the year's money and they panic. They don't know the cost of some of the simplest things like shampoo and toothpaste because they've always taken these for granted at home."

I smiled as he said this because I recalled the comment of one of my children in his freshman year who said with a tone of outrage, "Do *you* know how much laundry soap costs?"

Even more eye-opening to young people is their first paycheck. Seeing how much is taken out for taxes and other deductions, and realizing that what's left over must cover rent, utilities, and food, can be a painful lesson, especially for those who marry young. Many young people go from their parents' home directly into marriage and have never had the experience of managing even a personal budget. Severe economic stress in these young marriages can create a dysfunctional family all too quickly.

Parents who do not teach their children the realities of money are not preparing them for life ahead. I found that parents who tend to deal with money stresses most effectively are also those who make a conscious effort to teach children how to manage money. Teaching children about money doesn't correlate with the amount of money in the family, incidentally. I found couples in all income categories who saw this as a parental responsibility and others who didn't. When there's plenty of money in the family, some parents may be tempted to forego this education, but many other parents in comfortable income brackets insist that their children earn, save, and budget. In families where sufficient income is a problem, this education is even more urgent; yet some low-income parents do not want to worry their children about money, so they fail to teach them about it.

Children often learn that if they beg, whine, and persist in their demands, they will eventually wear their parents down and get what they want. Children's demands can cause great stress in the family if parents permit them to continue. Dr. Joseph L. Felix, psychologist and author of *It's Easier for a Rich Man to Enter Heaven Than for a Poor Man to Remain on Earth*, believes that one of the most damaging mistakes we can make is giving too much. "Overgiving deprives children of the desire to achieve on their own," he writes. "We must realize that we are really helping our young people when we don't give them everything they ask for. Teaching them to do without also develops a greater appreciation for what they have."[5]

Particularly destructive is the practice of buying things for children because "everybody else has one." Far more effective is a healthy family practice of forcing children to make choices: you can go skiing or you can buy that TV cartridge, but there isn't enough money for both. This prepares them for choice-making as adults. When they grow up believing they can have both, they will be resentful spouses, assuming that nothing should be denied them.

One of the most common practices among parents who teach their children money-management techniques is sharing with them the reality of the paycheck. "Our children know what our monthly paychecks are and what is automatically deducted," a mother said. "They know what our house payment and utility bills are. They know what we put into savings and what's left over for fun. We've found that knowing this gives them greater respect for money and diminishes their demands for personal items."

Another popular practice, and one I found to be very effective, is offering to pay a certain percentage of a coveted item, implying that if the children want it badly enough, they will work for the rest. In the greater world, we call this "matching funds"; a foundation offers $10,000 to an organization that needs help if the organization matches it by raising its own $10,000. This strategy eliminates the handout philosophy which is counterproductive in both organizations and families. Likewise, parents do not exist to hand out monies to children. A more effective way to prepare children for making decisions about money is to discuss with them the need and desire for an item, the cost range (which necessitates the child's skill in comparison shopping), the means of financing it, and perhaps the choice to give up something else to obtain it.

Ten-year-old Sandy and her family offer a good example of this process. Sandy wanted a new ten-speed bicycle. Her parents sat down with her and talked about her need and desire for it. Sandy already had a hand-me-down three-speed bike, but she really wanted the new bike in order to keep up with her friends on after-school and weekend rides. This desire seemed reasonable to her parents, so they asked Sandy to price some ten-speeds and report what she found. They spoke to her about the relationship between quality and price and also the temptation to spend more for highly advertised name brands. "Specifically, we explained to her that since she would be paying for most of it, it was to her advantage to shop long and carefully rather than make a quick decision to have her bike right away," said her mother. "I told her I would drive her to the stores but that she had to read the ads and catalogs and decide where to shop.

"We probably spent more on gas for comparison shopping than we did on the bike, but she became an expert on ten-speeds and found a great price difference in the one she wanted at different stores." What pleased them most was that once she decided on the bike, *she,* not they, suggested she wait until it went on sale. It never did, so after a couple of months, she said she was ready to buy.

Then Sandy and her parents sat together again to discuss the financing. They agreed that she could sell her three-speed and use that money as partial payment, and then they set up a loan policy with her, complete with interest, to finance the rest. She agreed to pay off five dollars monthly with an additional fifty cents interest charge. If she wanted to pay off more, she would not have to pay the interest.

She placed an ad, sold her old bike, bought the new one and looked for ways other than giving up her allowance to make her payments. Because she was too young to baby-sit and there were few other means of making money at outside jobs, her parents offered her some work at home at an hourly wage.

"But it wasn't make-work," her dad stressed. "It was mainly things that needed doing that we didn't have time to do, like painting some rusty lockers in the garage and digging up an old flower bed. It wasn't easy work but she was glad to do it and she did a good job." Sandy paid off her loan early and with great pride.

Although these parents were easily able to afford a new bike for Sandy, they recognized the value of the process they went through. And, while it would have been much easier and less time-consuming to simply go out and buy the bike, her parents knew that good financial education takes time and hands-on experience.

Other children aren't so lucky. They aren't given an opportunity to test their ability to handle money. They're given an allowance, perhaps, but little education on how to use it. In an article, "What Nobody Else Will Tell Your Child About Money," Grace Weinstein claims, "It isn't hard to teach children about money if we take advantage of their natural curiosity and adapt the lessons to their age level." She quotes John Holt who says, "Children are interested in the adult world and what's important in it. We should open up financial affairs to children, give them some idea of what's ahead. We'll find they are fascinated to learn!"

Weinstein writes of a credit union in Topeka, Kansas, which offers bicycle loans at 8 percent to children under seventeen. "With a maximum loan of $200—cosigned by parents, to be repaid in one year—the Kansas Credit Union hopes to teach young people about money management while building customers for the future."

Weinstein also advises sharing the relationship between credit and payments with children on a daily level. "Too often, when teenagers borrow our credit cards, they fail to understand the connection between incurring bills and paying them. It's up to us to show them that relationship. If you allow your ten-year-old to charge school lunches at the local luncheonette, take him with you when you pay the bill. When you shop for your child's school clothes and put the purchase on your department store charge account, show him the bill when it comes in. If you leave the dentist's office without paying for the visit, explain to your child that a bill will be sent and show it to him when it arrives. In each case, you can combine a lesson on credit with a lesson on checking and have your child write the checks that will pay these bills."[16]

Dr. Felix holds that all lessons pertaining to money should be positive and constructive. "Too often we let our children see us fretting over problems of inflation and economic shortage," he writes. "The message we give them is that money is one of the most important things in life and we know that's not true. Whether our children learn to love is much more important than whether they learn to balance a budget. We need to teach them not to overvalue money."

How do we teach them this? "Ideally, we want our children to see money as an extension of themselves, a resource that can go in their place to help others. We want them to realize that they are stewards of their financial resources, charged with the responsibility of using them well. And just as you can't teach your son or daughter to hit a baseball by verbal instruction—you have to put the bat in their young hands and let them swing—you can't just talk about using money wisely and expect youngsters to learn."[7]

But where are children to get this money we're called upon to teach them to manage? Here arises the continuing dilemma of parents: should children be given an allowance, be paid for chores, or be given money when they need it, or should parents use a combination of these three most popular methods of putting money into the hands of children? Curiously, I found no one practice favored over another by parents in stress-effective families. Some give allowances, increasing them as the chldren's needs and ages increase. Some tie the allowance into chores. When the chores are done well and without reminder, total allowance is given. When they're done less well or reluctantly, the allowance diminishes proportionately.

Others decry allowances and insist that their children earn all their money by doing small jobs around the home—a practice some parents abhor. Still others do not implement any ongoing allowance or payment policy but feel more comfortable in doling out money as needed by children. What is evident in healthy families is that they are comfortable with whatever policy they choose and they make it work for them. "We tried the allowance system, but we couldn't make it work in our family," admitted a mother. "Either it wasn't enough to cover their needs so we had to give more, or it was too much and they squandered it, so we went to a system with a minimal two dollar weekly allowance and a list of nonroutine chores that they can do if they want or need extra money. For us, it's worked fairly well. We don't pay them for keeping their room clean but if they want to wash the car or mow the lawn, they can earn extra money."

The controversy over the allowance system isn't likely to be resolved, because each family is unique in its attitude toward money. And it seems counterproductive to argue over which is the better way because what works for one family doesn't work or another.

A single parent quoted in a *Christian Science Monitor* article sees allowances as a regular part of the family budget. "The children are part of the family and they deserve to have a part of the family income," she says. "When there is no money available—like the time we had to get a new roof—there were no allowances. They can understand these things; they wanted a new roof, too. They have a part in making up the budget and have a say in where the money will go."

Another family expected their children to contribute about 5 percent of their allowance or money earned from jobs to a fund for special family activities the everyday budget couldn't cover.[18]

Families who teach financial management often have clear stipulations regarding allowances or payments for odd jobs. Does the allowance cover bus fares? Are savings expected and if so, how much? What about school supplies? Are children expected to buy their own socks and underwear or only special clothing items? Clarifying such issues takes stress off the family, for they don't need to argue every time a spending question comes up. "Do I have to pay for it myself?" is a nerve-racking question frequently heard by parents who haven't made these policies clear.

I found that effective parents tend to be confident in their right to set certain stipulations on wages from part-time jobs and allowances. They curtail hours if the job seems to be interfering with school and family functions, and they insist that a certain amount of money be spent for necessities and that a certain amount be saved. Many of them require potential college students to salt away a good share of their earnings for college costs. And these parents do not continue to give allowances and other monies once the adolescent begins earning enough for his or her own needs, a trap that other parents fall into.

The number of hours worked seems to be another area where strong parents hold some control. They feel responsible in setting limits, particularly in situations where the part-time job becomes more important than school and friends to the young person. Ellen Greenberger and Laurence D. Steinberg, of the University of California at Irvine, studied work patterns of over five hundred high-school students and discovered that for some students, part-time work led to falling grades, absenteeism, and more use of drugs and alcohol. "It didn't matter what kind of jobs they had," they said. "The critical factor was how many hours they were spending at work." They came to the conclusion that fifteen hours of work per week for sophomores and twenty for juniors marked the cutoff point beyond which young people were likely to start having problems.[19]

Work can be positive for youngsters, particularly when it uses excess energy or fills excess hours often spent just "hanging around." Jobs can give young people an experience of the workplace—the importance of being on time, of getting along with fellow workers and employers, and of feeling accomplishment. Wages give them some pride and autonomy. As long as adolescent work and spending patterns are monitored by parents, part-time teenage work can be a beneficial experience.

To summarize, I was impressed by the many creative techniques families use in dealing with the major stresses that accompany money or lack of money. They feel they have some sense of control over finances, except in old-age worries, and do not allow their family life to be a constant battle-ground on which each expenditure becomes a source of tension. Rather, they develop policies and behaviors that eliminate daily disagreements and arguments.

In dealing with money, stress-effective families

1. talk about money,
2. do not link self-esteem with earning power,

3. develop money-management skills,
4. teach children about money.

5

Children
and Other Challenges

Children's behavior/discipline/sibling fighting was named as a top stress by 53 percent of married men, by 33 percent of married women, and by 52 percent of single mothers. It appeared fourth on the lists of both married men and women and fifth on the lists of single mothers. Overall, it was the second most-named stress.

* * *

Communicating with children was named as a top stress by 53 percent of married men, by 33 percent of married women, and by 40 percent of single mothers. It was listed third by married men and eighth by single mothers, but was not listed in the top ten by married women.

* * *

"Remember, being a parent is easy, until you have children."

—Anonymous

In a recent University of Wisconsin study, Professor Catherine Chilman found that 70 percent of the fathers and mothers studied in a middle-class sample said that while children present stresses in their lives, they are still mostly happy with parenting. Two-thirds of these 702 parents considered parenting as their major source of satisfaction in life, as compared with work, personal development, and other achievements.[1]

In my own interviews, I was struck by how much stress-effective parents enjoy their children.

They have problems and stresses with children, to be sure, but they like their children. They tend to focus on the rewards of parenting more than the problems. Their basic mood is positive, even in families who have experienced terrific stressors like a child's handicap, severe or prolonged illness, or adolescent alcohol and drug abuse. I laughed outright at the response of a mother of eight when asked how she coped. She replied, "I don't believe in coping. Coping is so dreary. I meet challenges instead." She smiled. "I guess you could say that I'm copeless."

One fact becomes immediately apparent among these parents—they like themselves and their roles as men and women. They don't compete for status or power in the family but tend to cooperate and complement one another. Healthy parents can be equal *and* different. They value the other's strengths and their own as well. "I hear other women complain about passive husbands," one wife said, "but I treasure mine. I am too aggressive—I don't need assertiveness training—and his laid-back attitude is good for us."

Another husband reported, "We're a good balance. I earn, she spends. I worry about the future, she says it will all work out. I'm basically pessimistic, she's optimistic. I get sick, she gets well. She really is something else. . . ." The love and respect shining through his words tell us that he recognizes the balance she offers his life.

Not that these couples have escaped the tension of changing roles in the last decades. They haven't, but they do tend to concentrate on individual differences and strengths rather than on societally imposed roles. In many of these families, for example, the mother is more authoritative and the father more permissive. But they especially value the differences because they recognize their own capabilities and limitations, accept them, and are grateful, not resentful, at having a partner who fills in their weak spaces.

These fathers like to be fathers, and these mothers like to be mothers. And both nurture and care for their children. They enjoy their roles in their children's growth and development. And they get a kick out of being with them. These are the characteristics healthy families display with their children:

- They enjoy their children.
- They have confidence in their right to parent.
- They have reasonable expectations.
- They spend time with their children.
- They choose a comfortable parenting style.
- They set clear but flexible rules.
- They communicate well.
- They are more interested in relationships than discipline.
- They are good problem-solvers.
- They minimize the strains of adolescence.

1. Stress-effective parents enjoy their children.
They don't see them as a duty or an extension of themselves, but as a pleasure. And in this, they run counter to our culture. In her book *Sex and Destiny,* Germaine Greer points out that we live in a society that is basically antichild, one that doesn't like to have children around and spends a great deal of effort in separating adults and children. "Historically human societies have been pro-child; modern society is unique in that it is profoundly hostile to children," she writes. "We in the West do not refrain from childbirth because we are concerned about the population explosion or because we feel we cannot afford children, but because we do not like children."[2]

Harsh words, but they bear out the experience of parents who sense the displeasure of adults in church when children cry or when they have to sit near a child on a plane; or who read housing advertisements that say "No children," or travel offers for "child-free vacations," or restaurant ads that discourage family dining. Greer says, "Restaurants, cinemas, offices and supermarkets are all no places for children. In England, restaurants mentioned in the *Good Food Guide* boldly advise parents to leave 'under-14s and dogs at home.' Their object in doing so is to increase their patronage by vaunting their child-free condition. . . . Adults cannot have fun while kids are around; kids must be 'put down' first. Drinking and flirting, the principal expressions of adult festivity, are both inhibited by the presence of children."[3]

Family therapists are applauding the decision of adults who don't like children not to have them, a dramatic cultural shift from the traditional view that all couples should have children. "Children deserve to be liked," one family therapist said bluntly. "Those who do not enjoy children should not have them because it's the thing to do or because their parents want a grandchild or because they think parenthood will change them into lovers of children. Some people just shouldn't have children, that's all."

Yet satisfied parents enjoy children. They get pleasure from watching them develop from toddlers to wide-eyed kindergartners, to snake-collecting eight-year-olds, to preteen sophists, and to emerging adolescents and adults. And their kids know it. Children who know that their parents enjoy them, not just love them because they are their progeny, feel secure and worthwhile.

These children are treated as individuals rather than as extensions of their parents. Mister Rogers, the gentle television father to thousands of young children, says, "If the day ever came when we were able to accept ourselves and our children exactly as we and they are, I believe we would have come very close to an ultimate understanding of what 'good' parenting means."

Yet, how to do this is a question that comes up over and over again in parenting education. A mother in one of my workshops indicated how difficult this can be when she wrote, "Can you give us some hints on how to step back and view our child as a person rather than as an extension of ourselves? We can't be cool, detached adults with our own children like we can with others."

We begin by liking ourselves, liking our children, and examining our attitude about what makes a successful child. I frequently begin an intensive parenting seminar by asking parents to list the qualities of a successful child. I consistently find two quite different responses within the same group. One type of parent believes that a successful child is judged by how much he or she achieves or how he or she turns out as an adult, while the other type values the child as a child, recognizing that qualities like self-esteem, carefreeness, awe, and the ability to get along with others are more important than achievements.

Pushing children to behave like adults often stymies their development as adults, especially as parents. Denver child psychologist Henry Fischer holds that the best preparation for parenthood is the feeling of adequacy as a child. When we deny children the experience of childhood, we deny them the very opportunity they need to gain skills, confidence, and self-worth.

Family counselor Sharon Epstein tells of counseling a couple with a fourteen-year-old daughter whose schoolwork was not meeting their expectations. "She had several *C*'s and *D*'s on her report card, [and] their disappointment exploded repeatedly into verbal battles with her. A key issue for Diane and Ben was their expectations for Helena. Diane admitted that she and Ben were proud of their respective careers. Hard work, good grades, scholarships, and their college achievements had paved the way to rewarding professions for both. Diane was fearful that Helena's poor grades would prevent her from being 'successful.'"

As is so often the case, the major stress was not the fact of poor grades but the tendency of the parents to make all kinds of decisions for their daughter because they felt so strongly about the route to success. "They were not allowing her to become independent," says Epstein. "For example, without talking to Helena, they had signed her up for a Saturday computer class and had offered her services as a religion teacher at their church. Diane and Ben just assumed these activities were good for her."

The counselor encouraged the parents to begin to give Helena some limited independence. While this was very difficult for them to do at first, gradually they were able to separate themselves from their child, and a follow-up call indicated that family harmony was improving.[4]

2. Stress-effective parents have confidence in their right to parent.

They are confident of their ability to handle stressful situations. They don't agonize before and after making a decision the way stressed parents do. They presume they have the strength within their own family and themselves to solve problems. Healthy parents expect problems with children, just as they do with the couple relationship, but they deal with the problems rather than denying them in the hopes they will go away.

Parents who lack confidence in their ability to handle stress complain that children take advantage of stressful situations, and they are right. Columnist Joan Herst calls it "child radar" and claims that all kids have it. "When you are most vulnerable," she writes, "your young one senses that you are not in charge and reacts to this by losing control of himself. His radar is activated and he behaves like a brat thus forcing you to pay attention to him."[5]

Children can sense when parents are not confident in their right to parent, and it makes them uneasy. They expect a parent to take leadership, even if they fight the decisions parents make.

Many parents today lack confidence in their right to make rules and decisions, so they postpone parenting leadership or assign it to the schools, churches and synagogues, or even to the child's peers.

Confident parents need not be autocratic and unresponsive to their children's rights and feelings. The healthy couples I studied are not autocratic in any sense. They listen respectfully to their children's wishes, complaints, and feelings, but they make the ultimate decisions based on what they believe is best for the child.

Confident parents aren't always sure that they're making the *right* decision, but they are sure of their *right to make a decision.* They don't abdicate when children or society object.

Family therapist Salvador Minuchin notes that the ideal family is often described as a democracy, but that some parents mistakenly assume that a democracy is leaderless, or that a family is a society of peers. He says that effective family functioning requires the differentiated use of authority by parents, and to carry out this function, parents must have the power to do so.

Where do they get this power? They accept it as part of parenting. They expect to make a bad decision now and then, but when they do, it doesn't shake their confidence in their ability to make future good decisions. They learn to forgive themselves for being imperfect. And, because they are constant models to their children, their children learn that they can also make mistakes and still be capable persons. And their children learn to forgive themselves for being imperfect, as well.

Being imperfect is relatively easy for parents. Admitting imperfection is harder . . . but not always. I don't think I ever felt worse as a parent than the time I ruined my sixth grader's insect collection. It was a school project, and he had toiled for weeks, collecting and classifying the insects (which I found in little glasses all around the house). He bought a piece of fiberboard and laboriously mounted and labeled each insect.

On the day the project was due, I offered to drive him and it to school, opened the back of the station wagon, and suggested that I, not he, carry it to the car. He demurred, but I insisted. I picked it up carefully, but its deceptively light weight threw me off balance, and I tipped it over and dropped it on its face. Insect parts flew everywhere.

There was a moment of awful silence as tears began to well in my eyes. My son took one look at me and said, "That's okay, Mom. I probably would have dropped it harder. We can glue the bugs back together."

We did, and we carried the board to the car together. We went into school together, too, where I explained to the teacher why "we" were late. I felt terrible, but my son gave me permission to be imperfect, a gift I don't always return.

Just as the hostility of the parents comes to the world through the child and the love of the parents comes to the world through the child, so does the confidence of the parent come to the world through the child. Confident parents, although unfair at times and wrong at times, give their children leadership and security in the world of family.

3. Stress-effective parents have reasonable expectations.

Family counselor Foster Cline says that behind every parental worry lies a hidden expectation. I suspect he's right. We worry about our children's friends because we want them to choose friends like we would choose. We worry about our children's physical appearance because we want them to be accepted. We worry about their spirituality because we want them to believe and worship as we do.[6]

There's nothing wrong with this as long as we are aware of it. Effective parents have expectations for children just as teachers have expectations for students. But expectations can be tricky. The ones we voice are not always our real ones. Sometimes we *say* we want our children to be happy when we really *expect* them to be successful. And when their contentment conflicts with our idea of success, stress results.

We *say* we want them to enjoy school and sports for the enjoyment of learning and playing, but we really expect them to make the honor roll and win trophies. We *say* we want them to like themselves as they are, but we really expect them to be as we would have them be. When they don't cooperate and change, it's stressful for all of us.

Healthy parents do not intensify pressures on their children. I discovered in my research for *Traits of a Healthy Family* that one of the hallmarks of a family that affirms and supports is that the parents are able to distinguish between *support* and *pressure*.

Stress-reduced parents recognize their children's limitations and avoid pushing them into situations where they can't achieve. They are satisfied with *C*'s from a *C* student. They expect children to live by values they feel are important, although these vary from family to family.

Healthy parents expect shared responsibility in the family, but gear responsibilities around the home to the capabilities of the child. They expect four-year-olds to act like four-year-olds and adolescents to act like adolescents. Unlike some parents, they don't expect their preschoolers to be neat and reasonable, and they don't expect their teenagers to be helpless.

They state their expectations clearly and assume they will be met without constant nagging, prodding, and arguing. Eleanor Berman writes that it wasn't until she divorced that she discovered the need for her children to play a more responsible role in family life. It was they, not she, who voted down the idea of a housekeeper and allocated cooking, cleaning, grocery shopping, and budgeting in the family. She says, "The only way we can teach our children responsibility is to teach ourselves not to do for them the things they can do themselves. We help them to become capable only by praise and encouragement, by giving our approval even when their efforts don't measure up to adult standards. We can expect them to do their share at home only if we make it clear from the earliest possible age that a home is a cooperative effort, not something that is solely the mother's responsibility."[7]

I love the story Foster Cline told of the first night two temporary foster children stayed with his wife and him. The kids turned up their noses at everything served at dinner the first evening, and when, at the end of the meal, his wife had made no attempt to offer them alternative food, they whined, "But what's for us?"

"Breakfast," she replied.

In the morning they lingered in bed, dawdled while dressing, and were in danger of missing their school bus. Dr. Cline came to their room, announced that the school bus was coming, and scooped up their remaining clothing and shoes into a box which he handed to them with the suggestion that they run to the bus stop. They stared at him incredulously, being unused to such straightforward action, but when they realized he meant it, they grabbed the box and ran.

On their way through the kitchen, they spied the bacon and toast, paused, and asked wistfully, "But what will we eat?"

"Lunch," replied Mrs. Cline.

That evening they ate all that was set before them, and the next morning they were up at the sound of the alarm.[8]

When expectations are clear and reasonable, children accept them. But when parents say one thing, like "We expect you to come to dinner when we call," and then practice another, like holding dinner forty-five minutes until they come, children realize these are not expectations but hopes, and respond accordingly.

Stress-effective parents are very clear in their expectations. They expect children to get up when they are called in the morning or suffer the consequences of no breakfast. They expect children to get their dirty clothing into the hamper or experience the consequences of having to wear grungy socks. They expect teens to come in at the time agreed upon or suffer the consequences of not going out next time. Experiencing consequences prepares children for the time when they won't have a parent around to serve as buffer between their actions and the resulting consequences. I found no buffering or overprotective parents among those who deal effectively with family stress.

Eleanor Berman's book, *The Corporate Family*, is excellent reading for both single- and dual-parent families. It illustrates the relationship between responsibility and self-worth, a reality I find much more in evidence in the single- than the dual-parent society. Children of single parents are proud of their contribution and capabilities if they were not forced to take on too many responsibilities too early. Which brings us to the issue of forcing children to grow up too fast.

We see signs of this pressure everywhere, and family scholars and practitioners are becoming concerned. Dr. David Elkind, author of *The Hurried Child*, says that children are growing up too fast, too soon. "Inundated with the notion that 'sooner is better' by the media, schools, and a society that places a high premium on early accomplishment, these children are plagued by a fear of failure, a fear of not measuring up," he says.

He adds that parents who push their children to give them a head start in our competitive society expect children to take on the physical, emotional, and social trappings of adulthood before they are prepared to deal with them. One consequence of this pressure is that children are now beginning to show signs of stress-related disorders and diseases commonly assigned to adults.

Organized sports, cheerleading, trivia bowls, and the like, which were originally set up by schools and communities to give children a chance to refresh and relax, have now become so competitive that the organizations themselves are taking a hard look at results. The YMCA has been a leader here, offsetting the competition basic in many youth activities with programs that offer children a chance to just enjoy playing. Dr. Elkind cautions about youth leagues: "Certainly children learn something—competence, self-assurance, teamwork, for example. But this is by no means true for all or even most children who participate. In addition, structuring sports and games according to adult rules negates their value as play-time. At all levels of development, children need the opportunity to play for play's sake because play is nature's way of dealing with stress for children as well as adults."[9]

The super-baby movement is another phenomenon causing concern to family observers. "Our son Edward is only one year old and already people want to make money off him," writes Susan Schiffer Stautberg in the *New York Times*. "Recently, I and other parents of small children received a letter importuning us to send our babies to a 'readiness' program that purports to prepare them for the feverish competition at the better nursery schools. The letter begins on a note of fear, if not terror: 'In the next several months, you will be forced to make a decision which can affect your child's future. Which school will your child be able to attend?'"

The letter went on to point out the "inescapable fact" that the "more prestigious" nursery schools receive about eight hundred applications for only thirty places, and offered, for a fee, of course, to, in twenty sessions, prepare preschoolers for nursery school interviews in much the same way high schoolers are trained to raise their S.A.T. scores for college.[10]

Not so long ago, I watched a television segment explaining a college for toddlers in California which parents and babies attend with the purpose of getting them a head start in child development. One mother of an eighteen-month-old proudly flashed cards at her baby, saying, "Pick Picasso." After a bit of waving about, the fat little fist pointed toward a Picasso painting, and the audience applauded. A number of other parents followed, proving that their babies were equally precocious in reading, math, and even operating a computer.

I was saddened to see babies not allowed to be babies, and the program reminded me of my early parenting days when the proudest mother was the one whose baby was toilet trained the earliest.

Dr. Joseph Procaccini, authority on parent burnout, claims that the most burned-out parents he has interviewed readily admit they immersed themselves in parenting and that they express these beliefs:

- The success or failure of my children depends entirely on me.
- Giving 100 percent every day to my children is barely good enough; it is what all good parents do.
- I will be seen by society as a fine and honorable person because of the effort I put into being a good parent.

Dr. Procaccini sees these attitudes in the first stages of parent burnout, what he calls the *gung-ho* stage. "Parents in this early stage often deny their own needs for rest and recreation in order to help their children," he writes. "They do too much for their children without expecting them to share in responsibilities . . . overenthusiasm is a trigger for burnout."[11]

Single parents, in particular, often put adult expectations on children because they need the help. Dr. Elkind cites the example of a ten-year-old girl who was expected to make breakfast for herself and a younger sister, get them both to school, do some household chores, defrost something for dinner, and watch over her sister. In addition, she was her mother's confidant about on-the-job hassles.

"It isn't that such children are required to do more work than generations before them," Elkind writes. "The problem is that the child is taking on parental responsibilities. Children of years ago worked hard, but usually had mothers and fathers to take on the real worry and care of the family."

He goes on to say that many parents, especially single parents, confide their worries about their love lives, jobs, and finances to children too young to understand. "People in stress are absorbed with themselves," he said. "So much time is spent in coping with the daily stress of living that there is little strength or enthusiasm left over for parenting. Many parents don't have other adults to talk to, to act as support. But it's a burden on the child to be the confidant. Nor should a child be the parent's therapist, pal, partner, conscience, status symbol, or surrogate self," he says.[12]

Balance, of course, is the answer. And single parents who deal well with stress seem to recognize the difference between capabilities and parental responsibilities. They don't ask their young children to take on financial worries or the parent's job hassles. They do ask them to clean up the house. They don't ask them to meet the parent's loneliness needs. They do ask them to be sensitive to their complex schedules. They don't make them responsible for the behavior of younger children. They do ask them to baby-sit.

I found that the parents most able to deal with childrearing stresses are those who accept their children as they are and let them know this in a thousand little ways. They acknowledge their peculiar interests as valid, like the mother who hated snakes but found herself with a budding herpetologist on her hands. "Everything inside me said, 'Why snakes? Why not kittens or baseball like other kids?' But snakes are his love and we've learned to live with them."

Finally, as accounts of rising numbers of suicide among some of our highest-achieving young people indicate, success as well as failure can promote overwhelming stress. Parents who recognize this reality and value a stress-reduced life for their children set reasonable expectations for their children and themselves.

4. Stress-effective parents spend time with their children.

Probably the most striking difference between healthy parents and others is that the father plays an active role in parenting his children. This doesn't mean he likes all the repetitive and sometimes demeaning chores of parenting. He doesn't enjoy them any more than mothers do, but he expects and accepts them along with the more enjoyable aspects of parenting, as mothers have always done.

Someone once said that fathers are a biological necessity but a social accident. He was speaking more of cultural traditions than family needs, of course. Throughout history, we relegated fathers to the role of providing physical rather than emotional needs and then resented them for their lack of nurturing and caring. We did the same thing with mothers but in reverse: we relegated them to the caring and nurturing roles and then demeaned their ability to achieve outside the home. But according to psychologist Herbert Hendin, "Society has been easier on bad fathers who are good providers than on bad mothers with successful careers because the American model of masculinity has not until now included being comfortable with feelings, particularly with those of children. Nor has the culture shown a realistic appraisal of the importance of fathers in the lives of young children."[13]

Happily, society's expectations of fathers are changing. Ross D. Parke, in *Fathers*, points out that a new ideology of fatherhood has begun to make inroads into the old stereotype. "No longer is the father with a diaper pin in his mouth a comical figure," he writes. "The ideal father of the newest fashion goes to childbirth class with his wife, coaches her through labor, attends her during delivery, and shares in the care and feeding of the infant, especially when his wife returns to work. No longer a social accident, many fathers are active partners in parenthood and a direct influence on their children's development."[14]

Lucky today's children who inherit such a father—and there are thousands upon thousands of them. These men are largely unsung heroes outside their homes, but according to research, they are richer than their own fathers for their parenting experience.

Stress-reduced families have fathers who spend a good deal of time with them, both because they enjoy their children and because they want to develop a relationship with them. Many had little emotional nurturing from their own fathers and missed it. Jim Breig, in a delightful article, "This One's for You, Dad," writes, "What I'm saying, dads, is that we're being cheated when we let society, our wives, our jobs, or anything else block us from knowing our children more deeply, loving them more fully, and letting them touch our lives more often. . . . If you can't change diapers, wash them; since you can't breast-feed, take over the spoon feeding; if you can't be home all the time, make sure your weekends are filled with rattles, Big Wheels, and Little League.

"Why make the effort? Because the result will be better people, kids, and parents. The family hasn't survived all these centuries because of habit; it has survived because it works when given a chance. And, when it works, every member grows as a child of God to become more grown-up in every way possible. Even dads can grow up by sitting on the floor and playing, 'Go, fish.'"[15]

Families with good stress-coping skills generally have fathers who are involved and caring. They aren't into strict role division: she taking care of home and child-related activities and he taking care of the garage, garbage, and cars. These fathers are very good mothers in a cultural sense. They're comfortable kissing a child's hurt or throwing an arm around an adolescent son in affection.

Much has been written recently about the way children react to fathers and mothers, but it's very clear that men who are not actively involved with the children before adolescence reap the results later on in life in the form of resentful or distant grown children, while those who are involved in the nurturing of young children build a warm relationship with them that endures all their lives.

What about mothers today who are pulled by the strains of overmothering or momism on one extreme and the world of work outside the home on the other? Many are filled with guilt, whichever role they choose, and life for them becomes a precarious balancing act. One mother tells of calling her baby at the baby-sitter's two or three times a day and cooing to him over the phone. Another quit her job as successful director of a large suburban library because the pleasure of work became diminished when she had to leave her baby with someone else.

Some mothers, such as those described by Dr. Procaccini in *Parent Burnout*, overinvolve themselves in their children's lives to the point that they become chronically disenchanted and even grow to dislike their children.[16] I see many of these mothers in my work. I will discuss guilt and other stresses on both the stay-home and career mother in our final chapter, but both roles contain stress, and, of course, those who juggle the two roles are often the most stressed of all.

Children in stress-effective families get a lot of time from their parents, but it is balanced between mother-time and father-time. When there's an imbalance, it's usually an underinvolved father and an overinvolved mother—neither of which is healthy for a developing child.

The need for unfettered family time led one parent educator to develop a basic rule for parents: "Minimize your problem areas. Maximize your time together."

Most parents would like to do exactly that, but where do they find this time? As we will see, couples are already harrassed trying to find time for work, time for one another, and time for themselves. Where does more time with children come in? One popular but deceptive response is *quality* time as opposed to *quantity* time. "We don't spend much time with our children, but what we spend is quality time" is a common rationalization of today's parents. This presumes that a child's needs can be scheduled to fit into our time availability. Healthy parents know this isn't always possible. Children need us when they *need* us, not only when we're available.

I believe the response lies in the distinction between physical and emotional availability of the parents. We may not always be physically available, but if we let our children know that we are reachable and available to them emotionally, they are secure in knowing we are there when they need us, even if only by phone.

Some parents who travel a lot make it very clear that they can be reached at any time by spouse or children, as do many parents who do not travel. Sometimes it's a hassle to furnish reachable phone numbers, but it's worth it for both parents' and children's peace of mind.

"I let my hosts know that I am to be called out of a meeting or workshop if there's a call from my family. If they can't understand that, I don't want to work with them," an engineer told me.

When parents are emotionally available to children, their children reflect this in less demand for physical availability. A parent who leaves work to pick up a sick child at school is giving that child a powerful message. A parent who abandons plans for an evening meeting because a child needs emotional attention is saying clearly that the child comes first. Parents who scuttle weekend plans because "we want to spend some time with you" tell their children that both quality and quantity time are important to them.

A letter to Dr. Lee Salk in his *McCall's* column illustrates this value. "My husband often goes to his office on Saturday mornings to catch up on his paperwork. Lately he's been taking our nine-year-old daughter with him. It's nice for her to see where her father works, but shouldn't she be spending that time with her friends?"

Dr. Salk replies, "I think it's wonderful for children to meet the people their parents work with and see where they spend their time. I have very fond memories of my father taking me to his workplace and proudly introducing me to the people there. Many children I know have set future goals for themselves based on their fascination with their parents' work and the pleasure that comes with being close to a parent while he does his job. Unless your daughter is being deprived of the only time she can be with her friends, I see many advantages to her sharing Saturday mornings with her father in this way."[7]

Finally, a word or more needs to be said on the topic of balancing parenting time specifically in the single-parent family. A colleague of mine expressed surprise that 14 percent of my divorced and widowed respondents marked "spousal relationship" as one of their top ten stresses, but I was not surprised that much, for two reasons.

First, a stressful relationship with a former spouse who sees the children regularly becomes an ongoing stress in the family. Second, the couple who is able to put their own marital problems aside after the divorce and support one another in rearing the children are giving their children the best possible parenting under the circumstances. Their children realize then that although the couple no longer has a marital relationship, they have a parental relationship that tells the children that their parents love them enough to put old hurts and resentments aside.

I found many healthy single-parent and stepparent families in which the absent parent was still an active caregiver, and in these families, children and parents were as stress-reduced as those in many dual-parent families. Urie Bronfenbrenner claims that the difference between kids of divorce who make it and those who don't lies in the support of the mother by the father. He says that at least one other adult needs to support the caregiving parent, to free him or her occasionally, and to interact and spend time with kids. This can be a grandparent, a friend, or a sibling, but the other parent is best.

Dr. Bronfenbrenner uses the analogy of the three-legged stool to describe the interaction that takes place. A stool can't stand on two legs, he says, and a mother and child can't operate well alone without another adult to take the pressure off both of them at times to dilute the intensity of the relationship.[18]

I found this analogy to be true in the single-parent families I studied. In every stress-reduced single-parent family, the caregiving parent spoke of an ongoing appreciation for the emotional support and physical time offered by either the former spouse or a friend or relative who assumed this role.

Single mothers without this kind of relief and support can become overwhelmed by the necessity of constant physical and emotional caregiving. They can handle the daily stresses, but when there's an unexpected stress, like insolvency, illness, or a child's severe or prolonged misbehavior, they may just give up. "I thought I had everything under control—finally," one mother told me. "And then I got a call from school that my son had been truant. I just collapsed. I said all kinds of things I shouldn't have said to my son. I was awful. I just wanted to run away, to leave town, and I really frightened my other children, too."

Another luckier mother with a similar stress simply called her former spouse and said, "I need help," and he was there in less than an hour. She explained that she can do this at any time and he's there because he cares about his family. "He feels this is still his family, even though we are no longer married," she said.

The need for fathering after a divorce is beneath the relatively new phenomenon of joint custody among parents. San Diego divorce lawyer Marcia L. Nolan says, "I'm almost a fanatic about shared parenting after the divorce. Children whose parents are sharing custody are much more stable, much better adjusted. I know there are some who say that people who couldn't reconcile their differences in marriage certainly can't share their children after a divorce. And it's hard to do that. But people need to be told they've *got* to do it. You don't have to like each other to be good parents."

She adds that when parents agree on joint custody, what they're really saying is, "Neither of us is going to own this child. It's not part of the household goods, to be bargained for and fought over."[9]

Whether it's joint custody or not, the attention and time paid to children by the parent who no longer lives with the family is directly related to the amount of stress experienced within the family.

Institutions are finally beginning to address the needs of children from single-parent families, and they are doing so in creative and caring ways, I'm happy to report. Dr. Dorothy Rich, president of the Home and School Institute, a nonprofit organization based in Washington that helps design programs for family involvement in education, says, "It is being increasingly recognized that the schools aren't just working with the child alone, they are working with the family. Across the country there are now a number of courses that deal with various aspects of parenting, and a handful of these focus on problems relating to marriage."

One of these is a course on divorce offered to junior high schoolers. The course is called "Who Gets Me for Christmas?" and was designed to help students better understand and cope with the problems which arise when parents separate. Games divorced parents play such as Tug-of-War, in which parents compete to get the child's support, or Nothing's Too Good for My Child, in which each parent tries to win the child's love, or You Spy, in which the children are asked to report on the former spouse's behavior and life, are all part of the course. The course gives young adolescents a chance to talk about shared frustrations, experiences, and hopes at a time when they, too, are beginning to date. "We try to show them that there are positive ways to handle divorce and that divorce isn't contagious," one teacher said.[20]

To summarize this section on parenting time, I quote educational consultant Berk Sterling, who works with parents to help them motivate their children educationally. He says that encouraging children to sign up for classes isn't enough. "We're talking time again," he says. "Time and a lot of hard work. And if you take the time, your children won't forget. What they'll remember most about their childhood when they grow older are two things: how much love was in the home, and how much time you spent with them."[21] Stress-effective parents would agree.

5. Stress-effective parents find a parenting style with which they are comfortable.

In addition to a balance of parenting time, I found a *balance of parenting styles* within the stress-reduced family. Parents don't have to agree on every facet of childrearing and can be very different in their approaches without causing upheaval and stress. This is contrary to a destructive cultural myth that says both parents should be either authoritarian, authoritative, laissez-faire (permissive), or democratic and that when there's a difference in parenting styles, children will suffer from inconsistency and confusion.

Repetitive studies show that each child develops a relationship with each parent rather than developing a single relationsihp with a set of parents. Therefore, in families with one authoritative and one laissez-faire parent, the child responds to each accordingly. Children may argue and negotiate a decision with a permissive parent while automatically accepting the same decision from the other more authoritative parent. This need not create stress between spouses if each parent is comfortable with his or her relationship with the children and if parents recognize the value of complementary styles of parenting.

But differences cause great tension among parents who believe that they should practice the same parenting style. Often a relaxed mother, for example, will try to interfere with the child-father relationship by softening the father's rigidity and/or urging the child's obedience. By doing so, she intrudes into their private relationship. She is not responsible for the relationship that develops between the two. They are. Left alone, they will develop behaviors, rules, and unspoken communication techniques that will serve the two of them.

Because parenting styles and children vary significantly, we need to look at these styles, their origins, effectiveness, and hazards. No matter how many books we read or childrearing philosophies we adopt, we still tend to reach for the style of parenting our own parents used—even if we didn't like it. So we come into parenting with a subconscious blueprint that says, "This is how we should parent." Some parents never get out of this script. When they try, they feel guilty, as if they are betraying their own parents. Others are more successful at creating a comfortable style of parenting which may be very different from their own parents' style.

Besides bringing our own parents' style of parenting into our marriage—which may be quite different from our spouse's parents' style—we also come into the marriage with our own personality. If we're essentially easygoing and flexible, married to someone who is more structured and rigid, and believe that we must adopt a similar style of parenting, we're setting ourselves up for stress and failure. We can't change our basic makeup, only our outward behavior. So we are constantly struggling with ourselves.

It's hard to feel one way and act another. I met an easygoing dad once whose wife expected him to be the disciplinary force in the family simply because "that's a dad's role." He repeatedly tried and failed. When he talked with me, he was terribly frustrated. He didn't want to be "mean," as he put it, but neither did he want to disappoint her. They felt trapped by the prevelant misconception that in order to be good parents, each has to behave in the same way with the children.

Actually, children are pretty perceptive when it comes to parents. They can sense when one parent is acting out of character, when he or she doesn't want to be relaxed or strict but is trying to be. This confuses children. It tells them correctly that pretense and lack of confidence are operating instead of honesty and certainty.

Let's look at the four basic styles of parenting: authoritarian, authoritative, laissez-faire, and democratic. Each has its roots in prior parenting experience and personal makeup. Each has strengths and drawbacks.

Authoritarian: Frequently called the traditional style of parenting, this style requires a high level of parent control. Parents comfortable with this style are most apt to believe that they should agree on every aspect of parenting or the children will play one parent against the other. Authoritarian parents tend to take full responsibility for their children's behavior and regard children's misbehavior and mistakes as their own failure. They tend to have a strong sense of duty, and they reward desirable behavior in children and punish undesirable behavior.

What are most children like under this style of parenting? Obedient, courteous, respectful, competitive, and eager to please parents and others in adult authority. These are seen as positive traits by authoritarian parents, and many children emerge as healthy and productive adults under this kind of parenting.

There are drawbacks, however. Authoritarian parents may expect too much from children; parents can be more concerned with behavioral symptoms than causes of problems; and methods are often impossible to apply with older children. Some children of this parenting style rebel, act up, and escape from authoritarian parents as soon as they can. Others may become overly reliant on external authority, rely too little on self-discipline, or become overly dependent on rewards.

Authoritative: While authoritarian implies a high level of parent authority emanating from the parent's need to control behaviors and events, authoritative implies a lower level of parent authority, blending children's needs with parental leadership. Probably the healthiest overall style, I found the authoritative style operative in most stress-reduced families. This style requires a high level of give-and-take. Parents listen to children more. Rather than expecting all their children to follow the same rules, they treat each child as a unique person with an individual temperament and needs. These parents are more knowledgeable about what to expect at different stages of development. They expect children to progress from immature to mature behavior, but with help. Except in rare instances, they set limits rather than nonnegotiable rules.

Children of authoritative parents tend to be more communicative, fair, self-confident, and democratic than other children. These behaviors can be seen as either pluses or minuses, depending upon one's point of view.

Drawbacks include occasional lack of leadership and confidence on the part of parents; the fact that children may see their parents as occasionally unfair; and that this style requires more parent-child interaction than other styles.

Laissez-faire: This style is often called "permissive" by those in our society who like more authority. Children raised with this style of parenting have a high level of control in the family. Parents who choose this style are often compensating for an authoritarian style of parenting which they themselves experienced and disliked. As a result, they refuse to impose many rules and standards of behavior on their children. They are more relaxed, do not see an infraction as more than a temporary misbehavior, and believe strongly that love is more important than discipline. They view childish behavior as appropriate to children, and so don't demand mature behavior. They set only those limits which are necessary for safety or health.

In a family where both parents are permissive, it is possible for children to grow up without standards of behavior. But they can also grow up with good self-esteem, less stress, and less need to please others. They tend to be unself-conscious, impulsive, and nonconforming. They can also lack self-discipline and be insensitive to others' needs, particularly their parents'. Sometimes they like themselves more than others like them. Again, such characteristics may be positive or negative, depending upon one's point of view.

Drawbacks of this style are obvious: parents can turn too much decision-making and leadership over to children; parents' own rights are not protected; children may need more limits to function well and may never internalize self-discipline; parents may underestimate their children's need for values, socialized behavior, and consequences of misbehavior; this style may serve as a cop-out for some parents.

Democratic: In this style, parents share decision-making and power with their children, who are seen more as equals in the family than as subordinates. Both parents and children share control. Democratic parents depend heavily upon consensus, family meetings where they iron out disagreements, fairness, and collaboration. Often the family is run more like an organization than a family. Voting is a common procedure to determine a decision. Finances, marital tension, or children's misbehavior may be considered family problems rather than parental problems.

Children of a democratic style are often organized, reliable, argumentative, righteous, manipulative, productive, and able to accept personal disappointment. They prize free expression and fairness. When they don't experience these in other spheres of their lives, it's often a rude shock.

Drawbacks to the democratic style include possible lack of leadership on the part of the parents; a demand for equal voice by children in what should be parental decisions; resentment by a family member who finds himself or herself always in the minority; overdiscussion paired with inaction; minimal individual problem-solving; group behavior that is prized over personal responsibility; and the false assumption that all of society operates democratically.

Clearly, each style has its strengths and drawbacks, but I want to emphasize that few families embrace one style exclusively.

Stress enters in when (1) one or both parents expect to provide a single style of parenting; (2) parents shift frequently from one style to another because they are unsure of themselves; (3) a new parent or stepparent who is accustomed to a single workable style enters the family; (4) a changing life stage requires a different style than has been working but is becoming increasingly ineffective; and (5) partners don't blend and weave the other's style in with their own.

Many of the stress-effective families I studied have parents with widely different styles but use them to their advantage. "She's strong on rules and I'm more relaxed," said one father, "but it really works well for us because we tend to borrow each other's techniques when we need to. And the kids don't expect us to react in the same way. Like, I'm apt to say 'sure' to anything the kids want to do but when she starts questioning them about where they're going and who with, I realize I'm too quick to let them do what they want, and so I support her questioning them."

"Have the children ever attempted to set one of you against the other?" I asked.

"Oh, sure," he said, "they're kids. But they know that when one of us gets too rigid or too easy, the other is going to put on the brakes, and they seem to go along with that."

6. Stress-effective parents set clear but flexible rules.
"What makes bad families bad is not neurosis or indifference as much as incompetence," says Harvard scholar James Q. Wilson. "When parents have an unruly, violent, sneaky kid on their hands, it is not because they like him that way, or because they don't care how he behaves, or because they have

failed to solve his Oedipal conflict; it is because they fail to tell him clearly how he is expected to behave, fail to monitor his behavior closely to ensure that he behaves that way, and fail to enforce the rules with appropriate rewards and penalties, promptly and unambiguously delivered."

These words stem from research done at the Oregon Social Learning Center, which has treated over 250 families with problem children.[12]

The words are grounded in common sense. In my work with parents over the last two decades, I have found that healthy parents stress rules while others stress discipline. The latter believe that if only they find the right method of discipline, they will have well-behaved children. But discipline by its very nature is a reaction to behavior, not a method of childrearing. Discipline is used when rules and behavior *break down*. It is a corrective rather than a preventive action. Rules are sometimes developed as a disciplinary measure. ("From now on, the rule is that you will be home by eleven.") But the best rules are those developed to ensure values, behavior, and routines *before* there's a problem.

In families with relatively few child-related stresses, rules play an important part of life. These rules are few but clearly stated and understood. When children violate them, they receive a consequence.

I asked children in stress-effective families to name some everyday rules, those under which the family operates normally and without question. Here are those most commonly mentioned:

• Everyone makes their beds when they get up.
• Put our clothes in the hamper or they don't get washed.
• Empty the dishwasher before I go to school.
• Don't dump books and stuff on the dining room table.
• Whoever uses the last ice cube fills the tray.
• Don't mash up the newspaper.
• No pop after school.
• I have to feed the dog before I eat breakfast.
• Do homework before you get to watch TV.
• Call home if I'm going to be late.
• Come in the first time I'm called.

- If we miss the bus, we walk home.
- We can't watch MTV.
- If we're late to school, we have to go to bed an hour earlier.
- Get a *B* average or I can't drive.
- No hitting.
- Bad words can only be said in the bathroom.
- You can't wear anybody's clothes without asking them.
- Clean up your bathroom mess or you have to clean the whole bathroom.
- Last one out checks the doors and locks them.
- Clear your own dishes and rinse them after breakfast.
- Put the basketball and bikes away at night.
- We can only talk five minutes on the phone. That's a drag.
- Fill the toilet paper holder or you're in trouble.
- Don't cut across the Johnsons' lawn.
- Keep your music low or turn it off.

Note how often these children added a consequence as part of the rule: "Clean your bathroom mess *or* clean the whole bathroom." Children understand that the consequence of violating a rule is part of the rule. Because of this understanding, parents don't always have to come up with a disciplinary measure, and that is stress-relieving. When families have to constantly renegotiate the rules and the consequences, stress reigns.

I then asked these children to talk about special rules: those that apply to individuals, to certain ages, or to special circumstances. They were equally clear on these:

- Can't date before sixteen except for a prom or something.
- I get my own paper-carrier substitute. It's not Mom's problem.
- I'm responsible for keeping the lawn watered in the summer.
- I get paid for baby-sitting on weekends but not on weeknights.
- The kids cook Sunday brunch and clean up, too.
- If we fight in the car, we have to walk home.
- No *R* movies before we're fourteen.
- I couldn't wear makeup until I was twelve.
- We have to save part of our money for college.

- The youngest kid gets to finish what they're saying.
- "Teenagers do not own the bathroom or telephone" (imitating parental tones).
- Older kids get to stay up later than younger kids.
- We've got to go to church on Sunday if we want to go out on the weekend.
- If we're too sick to go to school, we're too sick to play.
- Call home if we're with someone who's drinking and someone will come and get us.
- Our parents will pay for regular clothes but we pay for special ones we want.
- We do the dishes after dinner while Mom and Dad take a walk.
- Tell somebody or leave a note when you leave the house.

I contrast these children with those from other families who couldn't really reply when I asked about rules. Rules in their families were sometime things, unclear, and unpaired with consequences. When rules do not bear implied consequences, they tend to be regarded as suggestions. If children are expected to make their beds upon rising and nothing happens when they don't, the rule is shadowy. It tells them the rule really isn't important or that it is only as important as the parents' energy in supervising it. In families with no specific rules, parents are often run ragged by inspections, pleading, and refighting daily issues, and eventually give up. "I tried getting the kids to pick up their toys," said one parent, "but it was just too much of a hassle. It's easier to do it myself."

What parent hasn't felt that way at one time or another? Yet even though a parent may take on duties that belong to the child to avoid stress, the stress remains because it increases the parents' load and tells them they have failed. Compare the parent quoted above to the way family counselor Foster Cline handles a rule and its consequence for a child: "Do you want to pick up your toys so you know where they are or do you want me to pick them up and I'll know where they are?" When the parent puts a box of toys high in the closet or in the trunk of the car for a week, the consequence of leaving toys around is very clear.[23]

I found certain characteristics in families who developed rules, which lead to less stress in daily life:

- They don't set too many or too few rules.
- They are clear in the rules and consistent in consequences.
- When they perceive a stress, they develop a rule to offset it.
- They don't argue about a broken rule or engage in daily battles over it but expect children to comply or experience the consequences.
- They feel confident in their right to set rules.
- They gear rules to fit the ages and circumstances of their children.
- They explain the reason for a rule. It's not just a parental whim or need for power, but a need for smooth family functioning.
- They set rules for themselves and serve as models for their children.

Flexibility is another feature in stress-reduced families. Parents seem able to bend without threatening the rule itself. Bedtime hours, for example, are usually set in relation to ages in these families, but when a special occasion arises, parents waive usual bedtime hours. Or, if a child tries valiantly to get a paper-carrier substitute without success, these parents will step in and get the family to help.

In this way, they model for their children that there are times when rules can be relaxed without loss of respect for the rule or the rule-setters. These parents also tend to allow children a voice in rules and consequences as they mature. "What time do you think you should be in?" and "What consequences do you suggest?" are frequently asked in these families.

Dr. Lee Salk, in a response to a parent asking about fairness in punishment, replied, "For many years I've been advising parents that when a child violates family rules, they should respond by telling him that he's done something wrong and a punishment is required. This can be followed by asking the child, 'What do *you* think would be a fair punishment?' More often than not, a child's response will be to suggest a harsh punishment. . . . When children are allowed to participate in such a decision, they're more inclined to abide by it and experience its full effect."[4]

Even when our own children were quite young, we would say to them, "What do you think you should do as a consequence?" We dislike the word punishment and found that consequence was just as easy for them to learn as punishment. We usually asked them to give us three choices, and we would pick the one we felt fairest. Many times their consequences were more severe than ones we would have offered.

Once in a while, being normal kids, they would come up with nonconsequential suggestions. We stifled that temptation by saying, "I see you're not ready or old enough to set your own consequences, so I'll do it this time." But that happened only once or twice with each child. I recall the time two of our children smashed the garden while playing ball and ruined some vegetable plants. I was furious and even more so when they took it lightly. When I asked them for three possible consequences, they, in a spirit of lighthearted bravado, said, "We don't get to eat spinach for three years; we can't weed the garden anymore; and we don't get to look at the flowers."

I paused, anger battling with laughter, because their answers *were* funny. What to do? I said, "Okay, you have one more chance to come up with three consequences or you get mine and they will all be related to your first suggestions: you will have to eat spinach every meal; you will weed not only the garden every day, but the whole lawn; and you will have to buy fresh flowers out of your allowance every week." Surprising how quickly they came up with some pretty good consequences of their own.

Humor, used appropriately, is invaluable when it comes to dealing with infractions, misbehavior, and consequences. I found that families who deal well with the stresses of children's misbehaviors and lack of responsibility tend to use humor positively, while other families use it destructively in the form of sarcasm, ridicule, and humiliation. Humor used negatively exacerbates the situation and increases the stress level. True, humor is not appropriate in every situation, but if used properly and at the right times, it can defuse a great deal of family tension.

Dan Kiley, author of *The Peter Pan Syndrome: Men Who Have Never Grown Up,* holds that if parents don't establish limits and rules, youngsters grow up without self-discipline and pride.[5] Not only do rules reduce the stressors of everyday living, but they also lead children from irresponsible to responsible beings who can eventually live on their own with confidence. Having lived with rules, they can enter the college or work world with a degree of competence and self-discipline that they would lack without fair and reasonable rules in their younger lives.

I believe most parents want to set fair rules and to enforce them justly, but I think many don't know how to go about it. They may parent in reaction to their own parents' rigidity or permissiveness. They're not sure which rules are too harsh or which too lenient or when to be flexible. They don't have confidence in their right to set reasonable rules. They don't link consequences with infractions.

Some parents ground children for everything—for talking back, for missing homework, or for driving after drinking. They are singularly uncreative when it comes to pairing the consequence to the misbehavior. Stress-effective parents are very good in this area. When children hit each other, parents curtail certain television programs because the violence is rubbing off. When a child shows disrespect for a mother, she says, "You don't seem to see me as important so I am not going to see you as important for a few days. I want you to know how it feels. You can cook your own meals, wash your own clothing, do your own dishes, and eat alone until Thursday or until you see me as worthwhile again." When a teen stays out late without calling home, these parents say, "Because our worry for you kept us up so late, we will sleep in tomorrow and you'll need to get up early to do our chores."

7. Stress-effective families communicate clearly.

"Our family fights but, well . . . we fight different from my friends. They get madder and stay mad a long time. We get mad and then we have a talk. Sometimes I hate those talks but we always have them." These words from a thirteen-year-old boy are more profound than they seem. They bear remarkable honesty and indicate a strong level of communicative problem-solving found in stress-controlled families.

When I interviewed families pinpointed as healthy by professionals responding to research for my earlier book, *Traits of a Healthy Family,* I spoke privately as well as collectively with members within families, and the young adolescent quoted above was one of my most delightful interviewees.

He put his finger on a common practice in healthy families: The Talk. The Talk is a habit communicating families fall into whenever a stress threatens. It emerges when there's an adolescent behavior that's unacceptable and parents say, "We need to have a talk about this." It appears when couples disagree and they say, "Let's talk about this." It's often used preventively, that is, couples anticipate and forestall a stress by deliberately sitting down and talking about a developing pattern one perceives as a potential stress.

But there's more to communication than talk. Many families talk well together, but they don't communicate well together. They overtalk. They go on and on about the poor dog who didn't get fed because of a child's negligence. They talk about it at dinner. They talk about it at bedtime. They're still talking about it the next morning and the next week. Gradually their children tune them out, and the excessive talking becomes a barrier to family communication.

Family communication can be described in several ways, but I prefer these two: first, that family communication is synonymous with *family interaction*; that is, every bit of interaction within the family is a form of communication, be it touching, silence, striking, or ignoring. All of these can be experienced without a word being spoken, and all involve feelings.

The other definition I like is that family communication is an *exchange of information*. The key word here is "exchange," for it implies listening. When one spouse or child talks but is not listened to or acknowledged by others, the exchange is missing, and the unacknowledged person feels like a nonperson.

Dr. Thomas Lickona, author of *Raising Good Children,* writes, "Much of what's involved in raising good children comes down to communication. We show respect for our children by how we talk to them. We need to be able to communicate effectively in order to teach them the values we cherish, help them learn to reason about right and wrong, and let them know we love and appreciate them. We need to communicate in order to encourage their independence and provide them with guidance and control.

"So at any age or stage of moral development, communication is important. If our communication with our children is good, our overall relationship will be good. . . . In a recent study of 250 children, ages 4 to 14, almost all the children said they wished their families talked more. And yet when parents and kids do talk, they often don't get beyond nonconversations like, 'What'd you do in school today?' 'Nuthin.' Parents ask: 'How can I get my child to really *talk* to me?'"[26]

Here, in skeletal form, are some of the communication techniques and behaviors I noted in stress-effective families and which Dr. Lickona and others speak of in their books:
• *They communicate by need,* not by schedule.
George Durrant in a fine little booklet, *How to Talk to Your Teenager,* says a father told him, "My son comes into the living room late at night and lies on the floor by me. A lot of times we don't say a whole lot. Often I'm tempted to leave and watch the news or get ready for bed. But as long as that boy is willing to lie there and talk, I'm willing to listen." He concluded with this simple statement: "I've found that the only time my children will communicate with me is when I'm with them."[27]
• *They value the dinner hour as prime communicating time.* I can't count how often this was mentioned in stress-reduced families. Dr. Lickona says, "The dinner hour is a golden opportunity for the kind of family communication that draws kids out, deepens relationships, and makes a difference in their moral development. Not that dinners will be idyllic islands of intimacy, free of all strain and strife. But with a little effort, they can more often be a grace note in the day, an experience in what it means to be civilized."[28]

These families pay attention to what's going on around the table, too. Television is prohibited. The youngest child is allowed a full part in the conversation, if old enough. Complaining or whining for the sake of complaining is discouraged. So are struggles over peas and broccoli. Dinnertime is seen as a time to share, not to fight.

• *They shift from talking to listening.*

There seems to be a good balance in stress-effective families— no monopolizers or mummies. And they listen well, responsively rather than reactively.

• *They don't assume what another person may be feeling.*

They don't vocalize motivations underlying what's said, as in "Johnny, you're hungry. Get a cookie," or "Sally, you're cold. Put on a sweater." One husband shared with me his resentment when his wife tells him what he's feeling. "When she says, 'I know you don't like gatherings like this . . .,' I really put up my defenses." Stress-effective families rarely make those assumptions.

• *They affirm one another.*

Put-downs, humiliation, ridicule, and such are not acceptable in families with good stress control. Members of these families tend to treat each other with respect. They acknowledge sensitivities and do not take advantage of them. Humor is used often but in a warm, bonding way, not in a destructive form.

• *They sometimes—but not always—have a specific agenda.*

One family plays a special dinnertime game they devised. This is how the mother described it: "My husband and I both work full-time and find time with our three children very limited. Dinnertime is our time together. We all take a great deal of pride in our dinnertime game that we have lovingly named 'good things.' We start with one of the children and move around the table clockwise. Each child tells one good thing and one bad thing that happened to him/her today. The rules of the game are simple—you can't interrupt the person who's talking. If nothing bad happened that day, you can say, "I didn't have a bad thing," and the same for a good thing. After we've all had our turn, we rate our day on a scale of 1 to 10. Other children spending dinner with us have really been enthusiastic about this and most of our adult friends who occasionally have dinner with us enjoy playing the game, too. We have found that it not only gives us an insight into how our children are feeling but why. It's changed a hectic dinner into many a pleasant one."

• *They keep confidences.*

This practice is particularly crucial in good adolescent-parent communication. "I always know that whatever I tell my parents they won't tell the other kids or their friends," one young man told me. "A lot of my friends won't tell their parents anything because they're afraid they'll talk. Not my parents. When I tell them something, I know it's confidential."

• *They admit mistakes, weaknesses, and problems.*

I was struck by the number of children who told me their parents admitted a mistake in accusing or judging a child and apologized. This is a powerful message to a child and gives them permission to do the same without losing face.

• *They pick an appropriate time to deal with stress.*

Many families shared that they don't always talk about a stress *when* they're stressed but wait until the right time. Timing is important. "I bite my tongue." "Let's talk about this when we cool down." "We're too hassled right now to discuss this rationally." "Let's wait till after dinner." "Let me think about it for awhile." All of these statements are examples of the way families handle timing of communication.

• *They pay attention to nonverbal behaviors.*

A depressed child, a withdrawn spouse, a sullen teenager, a resentful parent—all of these signal to families that something is wrong. Healthy families are good at ferreting out hidden feelings and bringing them into the open with questions like "Did you have a rough day at work?" or "You look sad. Are you feeling bad about something?" If the overture is rejected, they don't feel personally rejected but wait until the hurting person is ready for healing from the rest of the family.

• *They empathize.*

In such families, transactions are warm and optimistic rather than cold and depressing. Members feel bonded and expect empathy rather than rejection. This expectation pays off in concern and action by other family members, which results in even more empathy.

Don Wegscheider writes in *If Only My Family Understood Me . . .*, "In a system where differences are seen as opportunities rather than as threats, members do learn how to protect themselves from being hurt or misunderstood. A healthy system does not guarantee continual pleasantness and niceties. On the contrary, a healthy system guarantees that the members will be intensely aware of the complete spectrum of feelings. So a member of a healthy family will not enter the world as a naive Pollyanna, fragile and inexperienced with conflict. Instead, a healthy family member will have many tools available for coping with all sorts of feelings. A healthy family member will have learned how to deal with tenderness as well as anger, fear as well as vulnerability."[9]

• *They reconcile.*

Healthy families develop a reconciliation pattern, and members recognize the cues to making up after a disagreement or a full-blown fight. They don't let tension build because of unresolved arguments. Nor do they designate one member as peacemaker: rather, they take turns in making overtures to end stress. This can be as simple as someone saying, "Here, I'll help you with that," or as complex as the whole family gathering to talk about how best to apologize to a member they have hurt.

8. Stress-effective families are more interested in relationships than behavior and discipline.

"I was surprised not to find discipline anywhere on your list of healthy traits," a woman told me after reading my book on healthy families. "I would have expected you to find that healthy families have good discipline."

Her comment points up our almost national mania for equating children's behavior with family health and for discovering disciplinary techniques that reduce family stress rather than developing relationships that prevent it. Almost all of the traits identified in healthy families are *relational,* and when they exist to a high degree in families, there's less need for discipline. Discipline is a tool used to establish and correct behaviors. When relationships are healthy, behaviors tend to be healthy. When relationships are not healthy, the best disciplinary techniques available will not be effective in establishing positive behaviors.

Let's look at the fifteen traits of a healthy family named in my earlier book:

1. Healthy families communicate and listen.
2. Healthy families affirm and support.
3. Healthy families respect one another.
4. Healthy families develop trust.
5. Healthy families have a sense of play and humor.
6. Healthy families share responsibilities.
7. Healthy families teach right from wrong.
8. Healthy families build a strong sense of family.
9. Healthy families have a balance of interaction.
10. Healthy families have a shared religious core.
11. Healthy families respect privacy.
12. Healthy families value service to others.
13. Healthy families foster table time and conversation.
14. Healthy families share leisure time.
15. Healthy families admit to problems and seek help.[30]

Note how many of these traits have to do with relationships. When a family develops even half of these traits well, they don't need many disciplinary techniques. When they can communicate and listen to each other, they are already offsetting situations which require discipline. When they affirm and support one another, respect and trust one another, and have fun together, they are building a family that doesn't have to focus on discipline as a way of existing without stress.

If I could advise young parents on one issue, it would be to focus on relationships rather than discipline. It saddens me to see them so centered on the right discipline rather than the right relationships. They want to know, not how to understand and build relationships that prevent sibling rivalry and fighting, but how to deal with those problems in a disciplinary way. Their goals are misplaced because they are looking for treatment rather than solutions. And stress-effective families seek solutions over blame and prevention over treatment.

Any parenting book with the word *discipline* in its title is sure to sell. We're a technique-oriented culture.

We can pick up a book that tells us eight ways of dealing with a naughty child or a disintegrating marriage, but until we can really comprehend what a good relationship entails and how to develop one, we will continue to measure our success by the outward behavior of our children or the surface trappings of marriage. It's possible to have a family with naughty children and wonderful relationships, although the idea is foreign to many. If parents can live with their children's less-than-perfect behavior while building enduring relationships, they are establishing behavior patterns that will serve their children their entire lives.

There's more to family than behavior. It's an important part, to be sure, and misbehaviors can cause great stress in highly behavior-oriented families, but if the strong traits of trust, respect, affirmation, and responsibility are valued and modeled, acceptable behaviors will eventually result. On the other hand, there's many a family who produces well-behaved children who ignore each other the remainder of their lives because they have never developed a warm family relationship.

Family therapists and columnists Carole and Andrew Calladine, authors of *How to Raise Brothers and Sisters Without Raising the Roof*, tell us there are three forms of sibling relationships:

Heir/Heiress: One child is the Heir Apparent. This child always gets the most love and attention. The other sibling(s) play(s) a secondary role to the "king or queen" who gets his/her way.

Peers: Each child is recognized as being loved and important to Mom and Dad. Eventually the sibs begin to realize they are important to each other and bond together into a caring family.

Competitors: A child can win the parents' attentions and affections by outdoing or outsmarting a sib. There is a constant sibling contest to see who will get more love or the best parent rating today.

What kind of relationship do you want for your children? the Calladines ask. "All three exist. The first is achieved by parenting a favorite. The third form keeps the siblings revved up, vying for parental approval. Achieving the Peer relationship requires much more patience, thought, and hard work. It requires parental know-how. . . . Of the three, we recommend the peer sibling relationship."[31]

Modeling is the most effective method of developing relationships. When parents respect one another and their offspring, children tend to respect parents and each other. When parents scream at children for screaming, they are modeling this as appropriate behavior. I found that in families where stress is high, parents often model the same behavior they hate in their children. Then when they ask for a method of disciplining children who scream, *I* want to scream.

Relationships take time. Marriage develops from a primarily sexual attraction to a deep appreciation, but it doesn't happen in the first year. Family relationships are so interwoven that they require years of development. Each parent must develop a relationship with each child, and each child with each other child. And each of these relationships will be unique.

How do families develop into relational units without a great deal of sibling fighting and rivalry which creates ongoing stress? I found that stress-effective parents offset the fighting and rivalry by

- respecting each child for his or her own uniqueness rather than evaluating one against the other;
- realizing that rivalry springs from insecurity and a demand for parental attention; spending time with each child, which reassures them they are loved and lovable;
- refusing to get caught up in the children's squabbles but making them responsible for reconciling differences;
- asking children to remove themselves from the family circle until they are ready to be respectful and caring;

- listening to children's fears, insecurities, and feelings in an attempt to make them feel better about themselves;
- building the idea that the family is a unit with predictable problems and strains but that it contains the resources to deal with them;
- being hopeful that their children will turn out okay and letting children know that;
- modeling good behaviors and good conflict resolution themselves.

Because relationships are more important than achievement and perfectionism to healthy families, they focus more on building good attitudes than on rearing children who behave perfectly. Behavior is important to them, and they deal with misbehaviors in a confident and competent manner, but they go beyond correcting misbehavior to examining underlying causes for it.

9. Stress-effective families are problem-solvers.

One question I asked families was "How do you go about dealing with a problem or conflict?" and I got few answers because families who deal well with problems do so naturally and seem to treat each problem as a separate case. They can't list specific steps they use when a problem comes up. So I had to rephrase my question to ask "How did you deal with the last problem your family faced?" This they explained with ease, and I found certain techniques commonly used within stress-reduced families.

Every study that has been done on healthy families finds they are good problem-solvers. Problem-solving ability is directly linked to the amount of stress operating within the family because unresolved problems generate more stress the longer they lie around. It's not surprising that the more problems a family solves, the more confident they feel in dealing with problems. As a result, stressful situations can actually strengthen competent families, a reality that led one dad to comment, "What do you mean, problems? We call them opportunities for growth." (His children groaned.)

I found these five shared characteristics in families who are good problem-solvers:

They deal with problems head-on. Stress-reduced families don't dodge problems or allow them to go unresolved, although they may wait for an appropriate time to deal with them. "We sometimes postpone dealing with a problem until we're less angry or more rested," a woman told me. "But we don't postpone it for long. When there's a problem it needs to be dealt with as quickly as possible or it picks up momentum —and tension."

Some families actually schedule problem-solving sessions when they recognize a problem that needs attention. They say something like this, "Everybody stick around after dinner because we want to talk about this car problem" (or the bathroom situation or whatever).

They determine who owns the problem. Foster Cline says there are two types of problems: the ones that involve kids directly and the ones that involve the parents. "When it isn't a parent problem," he advises, "parents should butt out."[32] This differentiation is noticeable in families that solve problems. If two children aren't getting along, parents may advise them on how to settle their problem, but they recognize the conflict as a children's problem, not theirs. Parents may have to take a more active role in problem-solving with young children than with older ones, but they still expect the children to come up with solutions.

Montessori teacher Betsy Hoke mentions a familiar situation: A brother grabs a book out of his sister's hands; she screams and Mom comes in, retrieves the book, scolds the boy, sends him to his room, and returns to the book to a smirking sister. Both children get attention from the conflict, but it is not constructive, for the situation is likely to be repeated. The real loser is Mom.

Hoke suggests a more effective scenario: Mom comes in, stands in front of the brother and sister saying nothing, but holding out her hand for the book. Eventually, the children stop struggling and hand her the book, whereupon she says, "Thank you for stopping the fighting. When you decide who wants to read the book, I'll have it in the kitchen."[33]

Such a resolution involves the mother, but tells the children the problem is not worthy of her emotional energy. The kids may keep on fighting for awhile, but each time their mother responds in that way, their enjoyment will diminish because neither child gets her attention.

And it leaves the solution up to them. This technique can be used in the dozens of daily conflicts that involve siblings. A parent can quietly snap off the television, saying, "When you agree on what to watch, let me know and I'll turn it on." A dad can hold out his hand for the car keys and say, "When you decide who gets the car, I'll have the keys in my pocket."

The second type of problem, one in which parents are directly involved, must be handled differently. Take another familiar situation, the child who consistently fails to carry out a daily chore like doing dishes, which affects the whole family. A parent can nag, scold, entreat, and punish, all of which increase the family stress level, and none of which is particularly effective. Parent educators advise that parents calmly name a consequence and stick to it, like "When the dishes are not done, you'll have to eat off a dirty plate at dinner." When dinnertime rolls around, the parent simply sets a food-encrusted plate and a milk-shadowed glass in front of the child. If he demurs, they remind him, as calmly as possible, that if he wants to do the dishes now, he can return and eat off of clean dishes.

Again, this technique can be adapted to many situations. When a teen forgets to gas the car, the parent can gas it and say, "I'm sorry you forgot. I'll drive the car until the tank is empty again and if you want to gas it then, you can drive it." Or when a youngster refuses to clean his or her room, the parent says, "You must like your room the way it is, so you can spend all your time in it until it is clean." No emotion. No fights. No parent stress.

Foster Cline tells of the father who asked his son to chop some firewood by dinnertime. "I'll try," the son replied in an offhand way.

When dinnertime arrived, Dad asked, "Did you get the wood chopped?"

"No, I didn't get around to it," the son replied.

"That's okay, Son. I understand. But get it done before you eat the next time," replied the father. The son had two choices; chopping in the dark that evening or in the early morning before breakfast. There was no blowup, no anger, no stress.[34]

Contrast that with the way many of us would react: "What do you mean, you didn't get around to it? You sat around all afternoon watching television. Do you expect me to go out and do it when I'm already doing everything else around here? You take-take-take from this family and—*don't walk out on* me, *young man* . . ."* The anger, blood pressure, and stress all increase.

The major obstacle to achieving an effective kind of conflict-solving ability is that parents don't stick to the consequence stated. Many parents simply *can't* put a dirty dish in front of their children and say, "Do you want a lot of macaroni and cheese or just a little?" Many dads cave in to a request for the car keys because they want to be nice and liked rather than firm and unpopular.

One feature of problem-solving that stands out in families with stress control is that parents control their own emotional reactions. These parents deal with potentially explosive issues calmly and rationally. Their tone of voice tells the children they have the situation under control, and children react accordingly.

Admittedly, it's easier said than done, or perhaps easier shouted than discussed, but parents who control their own emotions in conflict have fewer emotional standoffs with their kids.

They develop conflict-resolution techniques. I wrote of these earlier in the chapter on the couple relationship, so I won't go into them again in detail here. The same techniques that couples use effectively to settle differences—compromise and collaboration rather than avoidance, competition, and accommodation—are effective in family conflicts.

They develop rules and procedures to offset conflict. Stress-controlled families don't refight issues. When there's a problem, they establish a policy that eliminates the need to deal with the same problem next week. Let's take a problem that plagues many families: television viewing. In some families, this is such an ongoing stress that parents give up trying to establish rules and resort instead to daily arguments. Not so in effective families. They set up clear expectations and rules dealing with television. Some common ones: (1) Certain programs will not be viewed in the home at any time. (2) Television will not be turned on until the dinner dishes or homework are finished. (3) Children may watch only so many hours daily (usually varies from child to child depending on age). (4) When there's an argument over what to watch, the children solve it or the set goes off. (5) Television is a privilege, not a right.

Television is only one predictable family stress which I found to be offset by policies and rules clearly set and adhered to in problem-solving families. Other areas of potential conflict for which these families had set policies included religious observances, dress and appearance, use of the car, chores, and school performance.

I saw one refrigerator with this typed list:

Seven Commandments For Getting Along with Mother

1. Thou shalt come in when called or come in not at all.
2. Thou shalt put dirty clothes in the hamper and clean clothes in drawers.
3. Thou shalt not use swear words, including "My God."
4. Thou shalt put my scissors back where you find them.
5. Thou shalt not ask why when I ask you to do something.
6. Thou shalt fight out of my earshot.
7. Thou shalt turn down your music.

I suspect every family could come up with its own list, which would not resemble any other family's. When I laughed at the list, a child took me around the corner of the refrigerator to a list written in graffiti style with pencil and entitled *Seventy Commandments for Getting Along with Kids,* which included items like "Thou shalt make pizza every night" and "Thou shalt not say, 'How many times do I have to tell you?'"

They deal with problems as a family. If the problem is between parents and an individual child, the parents and that child deal with it. But if it's a family problem like general irresponsibility or unruliness, the whole family is brought in on solving it. In healthy families, children as well as parents are responsible for each other's behavior.

For example, when an obstreperous child makes dinner table conversation impossible, the parents don't deal with that child while the others look on with glee and urge the child to even greater entertainment. These parents ask all the children, "What are we going to do about this?" I was impressed at how effectively this works in families. I know it works in the classroom when teachers ask students to help deal with noise, unruly behavior, and cheating, but I didn't realize how well it can work in families until I interviewed some of them.

One mother pointed out, "Children want fairness, and when one child's behavior spoils an activity or produces an angry parent, it isn't fair because the others have to live with the consequences. So when our son Danny made a scene at dinner last week, we said to the other kids, 'How are we going to deal with this?' and they said, 'Quit it, Danny,' and he did. It works most of the time because a misbehaving child wants the others to laugh at him or join him. If it didn't work, they probably would have said, 'Go eat in the kitchen, Danny.' That's happened before."

Her point makes sense. Why should children's behavior be a parent problem instead of a family problem?

In concluding this look at problem-solving, I'd like to share the creative way one family solved the annoying problem of persistently late teenagers who claimed they weren't late but that their parents went to sleep before the curfew time. "What are we going to do about it?" the parents asked the other children. One of them came up with the idea of setting an alarm clock for fifteen minutes after the agreed-upon curfew. If the teens came in on time, they turned it off. If not, it woke a parent who then waited up until they came home.

"It was a wonderful solution," said the mother. "And we would never have thought of it ourselves."

As I said, stress-reduced families are good problem-solvers.

10. Stress-effective families minimize the strains of adolescence.

It's no secret that children add stress to a marriage and even less so that as they develop into teenagers, the stress increases. Offspring who for years have been a loving part of the family seem to turn into sullen and uncooperative adolescents overnight, and their parents ask themselves, "Where are we going wrong?"

The answer, of course, is that they aren't going wrong; they are probably heading in the right direction. In fact, if no tension occurs during this time, parents should question their parenting because, as psychiatrist Anna Freud has written, *"to be normal during the adolescent period is by itself abnormal."*

Adolescence is a period of stress in family life for a number of reasons. As I mentioned earlier, when the couple relationship is strained, adolescence can strain it further. Another reason is that the presence of adolescents increases financial pressures in families where they may already be severe. Teenagers eat more. They wear more costly clothing. They consume gas. They go to college. In short, they cost money. I notice a marked difference in grocery bills when our college-age children come home in the summer. It seems as if I take up residence in the local supermarket with the checkbook during that time.

Also, the adolescent is experiencing a dramatic change within himself or herself. Adolescents are becoming their own person, but because they don't know who that person is, they try on a variety of personalities, which befuddle already confused parents.

In a study of one thousand normal families (as contrasted with problem families) for a Lutheran insurance company, family researchers Hamilton McCubbin and David Olson of the University of Minnesota conclude that these families' most stressful period—and the time when family closeness was lowest—was when children became adolescents. However, not all of that stress came from changes in the children and their desire for independence, McCubbin explained.

Fathers tended to be appraising their personal and professional worth in those years and making changes; mothers often were entering the work force or trying to reestablish careers. The researchers also found that financial pressures—the most persistent stress on families—were heightened when children became adolescents and that families who had learned how to handle money experienced the least stress during those years.[35]

In their book, *Stress and the Family,* McCubbin and Figley tell of a similar study of thirty thousand mothers which disclosed essentially the same thing. The authors concluded: "Women with children under six years old and women with teenagers are under the greatest stress. . . . Those with 13-17-year-olds have the roughest time of all. . . ."[36]

But in spite of these studies and pessimistic predictions of adolescence, a puzzling fact remains—there are thousands of quiet, unassuming families who seem able to weather these years with a minimum of stress. The parents aren't professional psychologists, and the teenagers aren't paragons of peaceful behavior.

How do they do it? Often they themselves can't tell us. Many attribute it to luck, but I found differently. There are certain characteristics that stand out in the way stress-reduced families regard and deal with adolescents. Here are the most obvious:

These parents aren't afraid of the adolescent years but see them as a normal part of development. That attitude toward adolescence is distinctly different from the attitude of those parents who live in a sort of ongoing dread for years before their child even becomes an adolescent. Likewise, stress-reduced parents tend to enjoy their emerging young people rather than dislike them. Over and over, I heard from these parents the pluses of having adolescents rather than helpless children around. "It's freeing," said one mother. "You don't have to be guarding them every minute like you do younger children." Other parents, those with more adolescent-related stress, would disagree. Rather than decreasing, they increase their vigilance and, subsequently, their stress.

Among the healthier parents I studied, I found a basically more optimistic attitude toward adolescents in general, as compared with peer parents, and a very optimistic and hopeful one toward their own teenagers in particular.

These parents seem to understand what's going on inside the adolescent. While they may not be students of developmental psychology, they sense the need of the young person to find his or her identity and place in life. And they know that if the adolescent finds it in the midst of a loving atmosphere during the teen years, he or she won't have to spend a lifetime searching for it elsewhere, as so many do. I think it's tragic that so few parents are introduced to the *adolescent search for identity,* because they don't understand it when it occurs.

Basically, adolescent identity crisis, as it was called by Freud and others, is merely the search for oneself. As children, we are more or less extensions of our parents and families, but as we reach the early teens, we begin trying to find out who we are as separate individuals. We try on a number of different personalities. One day we may be cool, streetwise cats, another day, professorial intellects. Our parents and siblings aren't supposed to notice or comment upon these several persons who temporarily inhabit our bodies. When they do, we become filled with rage because our privacy has been invaded.

In *How to Survive Your Child's Rebellious Teens,* Myron Brenton writes that plenty of young people do *not* rebel extravagantly, in spite of popular belief to the contrary.

He asks the question echoed by thousands of parents. "Why do adolescents rebel at all? Why do they sometimes act so wildly and inconsistently? Because physical (hormonal) changes bring on a certain amount of agitation—and physical maturation seems to occur earlier and earlier; many girls of eleven are already menstruating. Because adolescents are caught between childhood and adulthood, wanting to be children still, safe and protected from the scary outside world, and wanting equally strongly to be adults, finally rid of the restrictions and containments of childhood. Such a conflict creates much inner tension in them and makes many a teenager seem like a whiny kid one day and a composed, mature individual the next. Mostly, adolescents rebel because that's how they cut the psychological umbilical cord that has kept them tied as children to their parents."[37]

How do parents deal with this constantly changing person with a minimum of stress in the family? "We just sort of allow our children to be themselves, although this isn't always easy," said one stress-reduced mother. "Last year, our 15-year-old son decided he wanted a punk haircut, which was entirely out of character for him. We let him do it, but he was obviously uncomfortable playing that role. And it was embarrassing for us when we went to church and our adult friends asked about it. Then one day, he came to me and asked if there was anything he could do to make his hair look better. It was his way of saying he didn't want to look or act punk anymore. I took him to the hair salon and they made it look a little better until it grew out."

These parents distinguish between early and late teens in their rule-setting and demands for behavior. This makes sense because teen behavior is becoming noticeable among those as young as age eleven today. Children in sixth and seventh grade are wearing makeup, dating, and going to rock concerts. Many expect and even demand the right to experience the adolescent life once reserved for fifteen- and sixteen-year-olds.

Because of the pressure of peers at this time, preadolescents are torn. If their parents refuse to grant them adolescent status, these children can cause great stress by their behavior and moods. Stress-effective parents tend to grant them certain teen privileges and behaviors at eleven and twelve while reserving others for later adolescence. Generally speaking, there are three separate adolescent stages operating in our society: eleven through thirteen; fourteen through sixteen; and seventeen on up.

The first is a preadolescent stage in which budding youngsters of eleven through thirteen are beginning to give up activities and interests of childhood (even though they may still enjoy them) and practicing to be adolescents. They may not feel the adolescent rumblings within themselves, but they attempt to imitate the behavior of older siblings and friends.

Parents who permit some of this acting out while curtailing activities like rock concerts and teen-style parties are able to minimize the stress involved at home.

The fourteen- through sixteen-year-olds are deep into peer pressure in late junior high and early high school. This is the time in life when they most conform to others. Above all, they resist being different and individualistic. When parents counsel them otherwise, they get confused, angry, and stubborn. Parents who understand their mania for conformity and accept temporary fads, music, and language tend to exist with the least stress during these years.

Counselor Carl Pickhardt says, "Because adolescence alienates teenager from family in this way, the young adult has a heightened need to be with people similar to himself who can accept and understand his growing differentness—and these people are his *friends*.

"For parents, this pulling away from the family and preference for friends can cause considerable grief. They miss their son or daughter joining in family events and may even feel rejected, as though the adolescent doesn't love them anymore, or at least doesn't like them.

"This is not true, of course. A strong, positive family connection is still vital to the teenager's sense of security and well-being, and giving first priority to spending time with friends doesn't mean he doesn't value his family. However, parents who choose to interpret normal growth toward social separation as a rejection of themselves, tend to resent, complain about, and even criticize the adolescent's friends. This is extremely unfortunate. In doing so, parents do an injustice to their teenager. 'You can't criticize my friends without criticizing me,' declares the young adult. And he's right. Who he likes to be with represents how he likes to be."[38]

At sixteen and the bestowing of the driver's license, adolescents change. Our society subtly tells them that they are deserving of more freedom, and they demand it. In addition to being able to drive, we also allow them to get jobs, which gives them more control. At this time, adults begin asking them what they are going to do after high school, and they must begin considering the answer, which can be worrisome.

While few will admit it, concern about the future is a very high stress from sixteen on. Parents who understand the need to relinquish more control and who perceive the turmoil about the future that their teens are living with are those best able to minimize the stresses of this age.

And now we are finding a fourth stage of adolescence, one that extends to age twenty-five in some families. These are the young adults who can't or don't leave the family because of work and money shortages. These young adults would have been long gone in another era, building homes and families of their own, but instead they are still under their parents' roofs and, in some cases, thumbs. Stress-reduced families handle the predictable tensions this situation initiates in different ways. First, they don't encourage their young adults to come home or to remain at home if it increases the family stress level perceptibly. Alice Ginott, a psychologist specializing in communication skills between parents and children, said parents ought not to feel bad if they refuse to allow an adult child to move back home. "It's perfectly acceptable to say, 'Although I'd like to help you out, I don't feel comfortable with the prospect of you moving back in,'" she writes.

But if they do move back, she cautions parents to be prepared for confrontations. "The child is a young adult; yet parents almost always revert to their roles as parents of a small child." She suggests negotiating a living arrangement, for example, expecting the child to take over certain household responsibilities, to call when he or she will be late to dinner, to contribute a percentage of income to household expenses, and to accept the temporariness of the situation.

Ginott is most emphatic when it comes to giving grown children money. Don't even extend loans, she cautions. "Dependency breeds hostility. Having educated your children, you may no longer be responsible for them financially. But what you can give them: your faith in their ability to make the good life for themselves."[39]

In distinguishing among the various stages of adolescence, families who seem to control stress move from parent-determined to mutually negotiated rules. No longer do they depend upon "Because we say so" or "We know best," but tend to invite young people into rule-setting as they mature. Most ask rather than tell their children about curfews: "What time do you expect to be in?" rather than "Be in at 11:00 or else." They aren't abandoning their own responsibility; rather, they are nurturing their adolescent's responsibility.

They also tend to set limits rather than rules. Limits are boundaries within which individuals can move with some flexibility while rules are more rigid instructions. "We give our teens a lot of space," one father explained. "We set some limits on behavior like disrespect won't be tolerated, don't drive if you drink and a few other things, but then we let them pretty much operate on their own rules. As long as they don't step outside our limits, they're okay and we're satisfied."

These parents give overt guidance on sexuality. They do this in a variety of ways, from setting aside time to discuss bodily changes, sexual feelings, and peer sexual pressures to being casual and comfortable in discussing their own sexuality when a television program or some other circumstance inspires it. However they approach the topic, clearly they feel responsible for presenting some kind of guidance—physical, emotional, and moral—in this area. "Otherwise, you leave it to peers," said a dad, "and it's too important to be left to the alley or streets." I asked him how he initiates sexual discussion with his teenage sons (he has no daughters), and he said, "You don't have to look very far for a reason—a movie, a newspaper story, a commercial—sex is everywhere you look. We had a series of sexual assaults in our community and it turned out to be a 20-year-old who told reporters that he hated women and was out to get even with women for not paying attention to him. I just started talking about the story with the boys and it led us right into some pretty deep feelings and areas but it was good."

Another father said, "If we expect our kids to be open to their feelings, we'd damn well better be open to our feelings or they know it and won't talk. I tell my kids that I had some tough times in my past with my sexuality and we talk about it. When I admit to some sexual feelings about women as a man, it gives them permission to ask about feelings they have. Girls as well as boys. We put 'em all together. And my wife and I talk together with them—none of this 'I'll take the boys and you take the girls' stuff."

These parents accept and encourage their teens to hold different opinions from their own. They allow their adolescents more freedom of expression than do controlling parents, and by doing so, they assist their young in their quest for a personal identity. Although a parent may be unnerved to hear a teen question a sacred opinion—"I don't agree with you on gun control" or "I want to go to a different church"—this is precisely the way adolescents put on and try out their identities.

In fact, the more a parent cherishes an attitude, the more likely a young person is to take the opposite stance. Parent educator Carl Pickhardt writes, "One of the most stressful parts of the adolescent period for most parents is the dramatic rise in conflict with their growing child. They typically find themselves in greater opposition to their son or daughter, and for good reason. The teenager, in order to begin the process of separation which will ultimately lead to adult independence, begins to assert differentness in three ways. Through words and conduct, she makes it clear that she is now different from the way she was as a child, she is different from the way her parents are, and she is going to become different from the way they want her to be."[40]

Stress-effective parents don't equate dissent with disrespect as commonly as highly stressed parents of teens do. A couple shared with me the story of their sixteen-year-old son who suddenly began arguing about everything. "No matter what we said, he'd say, 'Well, *I* think . . .,' and he'd take the opposite view. At first we agreed with him to keep peace but that wasn't what he wanted, so we started arguing and he loved it. We kind of missed those arguments when he outgrew them a couple of years later."

Parents can expect their young adults to argue, and parents can expect to lose most of the arguments because reason isn't a high priority in adolescent discussion.

But even when these parents listen to all kinds of counter opinions, they don't condone or permit behaviors counter to the family value system. "They can say whatever they want about sex or pot but they can't do whatever they want with them," said a mother. "We draw a tight line between words and behavior and they know it."

It is interesting to note the style of communication operating between parents and teens in stress-effective families. They rarely use the verbal arrows that increase friction: (1) *The put-down:* "What do you know about it? The only thing between your ears is your hair." (2) *The command:* "You will clean your room right now because I say so." (3) *Sarcasm:* "It's a wonder Kissinger didn't pick you to advise him." (4) *Threat:* "If you don't cut your hair, I will." (5) *Psychoanalysis:* "You were insecure as a baby and it's still showing up." (6) *You always-you never:* "You always expect me to take you everywhere but you never think of my schedule."

These verbal arrows cut off communication before it begins and block the resolution of conflicts. Parents with good adolescent communication rarely use them and treat their growing children with the same respect they accord adults.

While adolescents may express behaviors and values contrary to their parents', the fact is that recent studies show them to be much more in agreement with their parents than were young people in the fifties and sixties. A 1983 survey of one thousand young Americans found that although they still show a streak of independence, they also exhibit some highly traditional views. They strongly favor marriage over being single, frown on marijuana use, and would like to see more respect for authority. An overwhelming 93 percent favor more stress on traditional family ties, and 51 percent agree that strict, old-fashioned upbringing and discipline are still the best way to rear children.[41]

These parents confront their adolescents only on issues of importance. No matter how well the family communicates, there are bound to be confrontations over friends, school, work, appearance, and behavior. In highly stressed families, every issue evolves into an explosive confrontation.

Healthy parents tend to reserve confrontation for important issues and give in on minor issues. "We don't make an issue of things like messy rooms and rock music because they aren't that important," said one couple. "But we do keep watch over the friends they choose and their school performance. We don't give in very often on those. The other things aren't that significant to us, so we don't confront them about those as much."

These parents monitor their adolescents' friends and other influences more closely than stressed parents. They know their teens' friends and welcome them into their homes to observe as well as to enjoy them. "Our son and his gang play poker," said a dad, "and a lot of the boys' parents don't like them at their home because they're loud and they wipe out the refrigerator. But we're just the opposite. We let them come whenever they want because it gives us a chance to see what kind of kids they are."

I found that parents who seem to get along smoothly with their teens enjoy their friends more, too. They are interested in their activities, know their names, talk with them about their interests, and view them as an important part of their youth's life, while other parents take a more ambivalent attitude toward peers until there's trouble or undesirable behavior.

"Know your kids' friends and you know what's going on with your kid," a school counselor said. "Remember that kids pick their friends for a reason. That reason can be good or it can be bad but you won't know until you know their friends—really know them."

What about the youth who chooses friends who behave contrary to the family's values? How do stress-effective parents deal with that issue? I asked parents. "Gingerly," responded one. "If you say, 'Get rid of that friend,' you're setting up a no-win confrontation. We set some rules like 'You can see him at school or here at home but not on weekends.' We've gone through this with three kids and let me tell you, it isn't easy. But we let them know we care about the kind of kids they hang out with and eventually it pays off." Many parents deal with the issue of inappropriate friends in the same fashion—they allow them within certain time and space limits.

Carl Pickhardt advises, "What parents need to do is not panic when a particular group of friends represents behavior they do not like. Opposing that social association often arouses opposition in the teenager, and causes her to rebel into a relationship she would probably have soon given up on her own anyway. Forbidden friends become highly attractive. Better for parents to accept the friends, and encourage their teenager to invite them over. Getting to know these new companions helps parents better perceive who their child is spending time with. Parents can then, without evaluating the friends as people, express concern to their teenager about the behavior of those friends. 'We like your friends, but we don't want you going out, getting drunk, and into trouble the way they sometimes do.'"[42]

In the article "Parents VS. Peers," Philip B. Taft, Jr., gives parents some valuable tips on how to respond to teenagers' typical arguments:

"Kids say: 'Everybody's doing it.'
Parents say: 'You're not everybody; you're somebody special.'
Kids say: 'You want me to be weird.'
Parents say: 'I want you to be yourself. What's so weird about that?'
Kids say: 'But we can afford it.'
Parents say: 'We can afford it, but we don't need it.'
Kids say: 'You're treating me like a child!'
Parents say: 'No, I'm treating you like a person your age.'
Kids say: 'Don't you want me to be one of the gang?'
Parents say: 'I'd rather you were one of a kind.'
Kids say: 'You're old-fashioned!'
Parents say: 'And more experienced.'
Kids say: 'You don't trust me.'
Parents say: 'I do trust you, but I'm not sure you fully understand the situation.'
Kids say: 'You hate my friends!'
Parents say: 'No, I love you.'"[43]

These parents tend to spend time individually with their adolescents. This response from stress-reduced families is so prevalent that it should be heard by all parents. These parents fish or shop or bike or cook or walk alone with each youth.

"It gives us a chance to talk" is a comment I heard over and over.

I personally relate to the value of alone time with adolescents and young adults. When I really want to hear my daughter, we go to lunch where we aren't interrupted by siblings or the phone. My husband frequently takes a son alone to a game, to an auto show, or fishing, where exchange of ideas and feelings are freer than when both boys are there.

While this requires a good deal of parent time, one of the most common therapeutic prescriptions offered by family counselors in parent-teen standoffs is that of getting one parent and one teen together in an activity outside the home. Why pay for this counsel when the prescription is so easy and so effective?

"Whenever friction starts to build, I ask my boy if he wants to go to a ball game," one dad said. "We don't talk a lot but just shouting at a referee together brings us closer. And the next day is better than the day before."

Finally, these parents help their children to leave home— emotionally as well as physically. They realize the pressures of separation—choosing a job or school, loneliness, dependency, survival—and they help their children anticipate these *before* they leave. Lack of guidance in these areas is a major cause of the postponed nest-leaving we are beginning to witness. Although youth may not admit it, many are afraid of life outside the comfortable cocoon of home. Many young people don't want to live on bologna. They don't want to do their own laundry. They don't want to make new friends or establish other support systems. They don't want to stay on a job they need but dislike. In short, they want to continue the dependency of childhood without giving up the independency of adulthood. This creates mammoth tensions in some families.

Or young people may feel their parents' reluctance at letting them go and feel guilty if they leave. So they leave but are emotionally tied to home in an unhealthy way. This emotional drain on their energy often gets in the way of establishing themselves in the adult world. Some pop in and out of the nest, coming home when they lose a job or room-mate, going back out when things get tense between them-selves and their parents.

I found that stress-reduced parents are very good at letting their children go and giving them confidence that they can make it in the world away from home, even though there will be some tough times. This difference in families shows up in the pattern of leave-taking. In families that don't let go, *all* the young adults seem to vacillate in and out, while in other families, *none* of the young adults do. How well the parents prepare their adolescents for life on their own is probably the major tool for evaluating overall parenting success. Stress-effective parents do it well.

In dealing with children, stress-effective parents
1. enjoy their children,
2. have confidence in their right to parent,
3. have reasonable expectations,
4. spend time with their children,
5. choose a comfortable parenting style,
6. set clear but flexible rules,
7. communicate well,
8. are more interested in relationships than discipline,
9. are good problem-solvers,
10. minimize the strains of adolescence.

6

Never Enough Time

Four of the top ten family stresses have to do with lack of time. *Insufficient couple time* was named as a top stress by 58 percent of married women and 52 percent of married men surveyed. *Insufficient "me" time* was named as a top stress by 29 percent of married men, 40 percent of married women, and 66 percent of single mothers. *Insufficient family playtime* was named as a top stress by 29 percent of married men, 37 percent of married women, and 40 percent of single mothers. *Overscheduled family calendar* was named by 39 percent of married men, 32 percent of married women, and 20 percent of single mothers.

* * *

"We don't have time for stress. We barely see each other."

—Survey comment from a married woman

The number of hours available per day is the one resource we all have in common. Other stresses stem from widely varying sources: income, work, size of family, ethnic makeup, communication patterns, and parenting styles. But time is the common denominator. We all have the same 24 hours daily, 7 days weekly, and 365 days yearly. Why is it, then, when we begin equally, that some families feel in control of time, while others feel controlled by it?

Practically every study and survey on family stress puts time pressures near the top. A 1981 study of over eleven hundred working parents by pollster Louis Harris found that 63 percent of working mothers and 40 percent of working fathers said they didn't have enough time for themselves. The same survey revealed that 26 percent felt a lack of time with their children and with each other. The same basic complaints emerged from my research.

In an editorial in *The New Relationships*, we read, "What workers throughout the global economy want most is fewer work hours. Five days a week they get up, make breakfast, eat, rush the kids to school or sitter, fight traffic to work; then, more than eight hours later, they reverse the process: fight traffic to pick up the kids, rush to get home, make dinner, eat, clean up and collapse. On Saturday, they shop, clean the house, do the laundry, and run errands accumulated during the week. That leaves just one day a week for what is most important to them: time with mates, children, friends, and self."[1]

One reason time pressures are so significant in any look at family stress is that, like a poor spousal relationship, they generate and intensify other stresses. When a couple suffers from lack of time together, communication suffers. When communication suffers, couples are less able to deal with issues like children's behavior and financial worries. When personal time gets squeezed out by work, family, and excessive community activities, predictable feelings like fatigue, tension, and a sense of futility give rise to sharp retorts, temperamental outbursts, and an atmosphere of walking-on-eggs in the home. "I wrote myself a note to water the petunias when I got home," said one woman. "Then after a full day of running errands and picking up kids and delivering them and having absolutely no time for myself, I got home and saw the note. I didn't recognize my own handwriting and blew up, thinking my husband wrote it. I tell you, things were tense for awhile."

When work or activities begin to consume a father's time, for example, his wife and children may feel neglected and resentful and begin to resort to passive aggressive behavior patterns that make his life more difficult. His wife "forgets" to put gas in the car. His children "forget" to kiss him good night. This is the only way they know how to do battle for his attention.

Yet this bleak scenario is not enacted in all homes. Many families develop creative techniques for allocating time and do find couple, personal, and family time to enjoy. They recognize time as a resource which is controllable, but they also realize that it's an area of family life that demands attention or it will get out of control in a surprisingly short while.

In an article, "Making the Family Work," clinical psychologist Stephen A. Timm explains the change in cultural use of time today as compared with earlier eras.

"Industrial and technological changes have transformed the *Little House on the Prairie* family. Parents who work rarely work at home; urbanization has separated work from home. Parents frequently must work 50 hours a week, including the time getting to and from work. More and more mothers are traveling the commuter trail. . . . Not surprisingly, because of these changes some unique problems and challenges face dual and single working parents."[1]

In addition to the change in work patterns, we have added personal development, children's activities, and community service to the list of responsibilities "good" parents should assume. One woman said ruefully, "I'm supposed to spend an hour on exercise daily, an hour meditating daily, an hour with each of my children daily, an hour reading up on world affairs daily, and at least four quality hours with my husband in the evening. While doing this I'm expected to keep a lovely clean home, cook inexpensive nutritious gourmet meals from scratch, volunteer as room mother, den mother, and earth mother, turning over my compost pile daily, and hold down a job so I can be fulfilled. Of course, I'm smiling all the time I'm accomplishing this." She wasn't smiling as she said it.

Columnist Bob Greene coined the phrase "the Twitching of America" to describe our national frenzy to save time. He tells of a restaurant that brings the luncheon tab along with the meal because people get impatient if they have to wait two or three minutes for the bill. "The so-called laid-back days of our society are definitely over," he rues. "The Twitching of America is claiming more victims everyday; no one really enjoys it, but the inroads it is making are undeniable."[3]

Newspapers and magazines reveal this twitching with articles about children who now carry bleepers, once reserved for doctors, so they can be called in from play by busy parents. And ads for waterproof rush-hour clocks to hang in the shower evidence our frenetic pace, as do adults who try to stretch their twenty-four daily hours by sacrificing sleep or lunch rather than examining overly busy schedules. I regret the twitching every time I read statistics on increased signs of pressure among children—ulcers, migraines, suicides—and on movements that push children into college before they're out of diapers.

Bob Greene concludes, "There is undeniably something deeply unhealthy about all this; a society that has begun to value the clock so highly has got to be missing out on certain other aspects of a normal life. The cliché, of course, is 'Stop and smell the roses'; now, not only have people ceased stopping to smell the roses—they resent it if someone who *is* smelling the roses happens to block their path on the sidewalk for three seconds."[4]

But while we may regret the pace of the society in which we live, we must live in it. How do healthy families learn to control time so that it doesn't become a stress that affects their personal and family lives? I've found that these families tend to share the following characteristics:

• They view time as a controllable commodity.
• They balance work and family life.
• They balance couple and personal time.
• They recognize their stress level and take early steps to counter it.
• They play together.
• They prioritize activities.

1. Healthy families view time as a controllable commodity.

People who have the most control and least stress over time are those who recognize it as a resource that needs the same attention as money in their home. So they tend to use the same techniques in managing time as they do in managing money: talking about it; sharing feelings and needs that arise from insufficient personal, couple, and family time; allocating time for certain activities; budgeting time; and prioritizing activities that eat up time. Some even have a savings plan for time—reserving time on their calendars for unscheduled needs.

Ironically, all of this planning takes time; but it pays off. Just as these families sit together to go over bills and checkbooks, they sit together and go over calendars, both weekly and long-range. In *Traits of a Healthy Family,* in which I deal with time in relationship to family activities, I found that the families most in control are likely to keep a family calendar and individual calendars—yes, young children, too—that they go over together once weekly.

During these weekly meetings, they focus on the amount of time they will have to eat together and see one another in the upcoming week. If the schedule looks impossible, they try to find ways of moving or eliminating some activities. In short, they pay attention to their time allocation *before* time squeezes become pressures that affect family relationships and harmony.[5]

In the first chapter of this book, I listed signs of a constantly stressful family, indicating that while all families experience stress to some degree, some families live with stress at a peak level constantly. I invite readers to study that list again, this time with an eye toward the role time plays in family stress. Here are the signs:

- a constant sense of urgency; no time to release and relax
- tension that underlies and causes sharp words, sibling fighting, misunderstandings
- a mania to escape—to one's room, car, garage, away

- a feeling that time is passing too quickly; children are growing up too fast
- a nagging desire for a simpler life; constant talk about times that were or will be simpler
- little "me" or couple time
- a pervasive sense of guilt for not being and doing everything to and for all the people in our lives—our family, fellow workers, church, and community

When I asked people to study these signs and respond to questions about them, I found that those least buffeted by time pressures recognized that the signs were a *result* of inattention while those who acknowledge living with these at a high level tend to see them as a *cause* of daily stress and feel powerless in controlling them. Highly stressed people tend to seek a place to lay blame (the job, school, latest activity), while stress-effective people tend to seek solutions (budgeting time or prioritizing activities).

Blaming is an easy trap to fall into because it alleviates personal guilt, at least temporarily. I recently directed two workshops at a conference center a couple of hours from home. One was held on Wednesday and the other on Friday, and both required a lot of energy and attention. But instead of giving myself Thursday to relax, I filled it with meetings, figuring it would save me a couple of trips later on.

My schedule was brutal, and I found myself complaining to whoever would listen. Finally, one good friend at the center said gently, "But you scheduled yourself." She was right. I knew that, of course, and recognized my foolishness, but it was more comfortable blaming those nonexistent *theys* than admitting I was at fault.

I find the same habit in many families who complain about time. They overschedule themselves and then blame others for their folly. This is particularly true of those who work in the helping professions: church, social agencies, and voluntary organizations. Many of them feel ongoing guilt because they constantly sacrifice time with their own families to help other families.

Families who devote attention to time and calendars also recognize and resist the temptation to fill time down the road.

They realize how foolish it is to think that they'll work every-thing in somehow when the time comes. That's why, on a very practical level, most of these families keep a long-range calen-dar in addition to a weekly or monthly one, a practice which resembles long-range savings plans. They have learned from experience the pressure that can come from blithely saying yes to activities four or five months ahead because the calen-dar is clean.

"We started keeping a yearly calendar after one disastrous summer when we had so many houseguests we didn't have any time just for us," one couple reported. "We were trying to work, cook, and entertain, and somewhere in there we lost our own family. We still refer to it as *that summer* and everybody knows which one. Now if somebody writes that they're com-ing, we look at the calendar to see if it's a good time for us to invite them. If not, we tell them we're sorry we can't offer them sleeping space but invite them for a cookout instead."

This kind of attention to family needs and time gives couples control over discretionary time. But it doesn't hap-pen by chance. It requires constant mindfulness and courage, too. It isn't always easy to write to an old friend who is going to be vacationing in the area and say, "Sorry, we can't put your family up for a couple of weeks because our own family needs come first." Many cannot do this. They invite the family and resent the time and intrusion into their own fam-ily lives. This adds to everyone's stress level, and they end up blaming the visitors rather than themselves.

2. Stress-controlled families balance work and family life.

In researching my earlier book, I learned that one of the traits of a healthy family is a *balance of interaction among mem-bers.* That is, strong families tend to spend proportionate amounts of time with one another. In some dysfunctional families we find cliques, subgroups, father/daughter dyads, and the like. But the most common imbalance reported in American families involves the overworking father. He is the one with whom children and wives spend the least amount of time. Statistics indicate this can be as little as twenty minutes weekly.

Work could take up an entire chapter, but I put it here because its stressful impact on family comes from the time pressures involved. In some families, the struggle over time becomes a battle with the workplace for the physical and emotional presence of the working parent or parents.

Barrie S. Greiff, who has taught a course called "The Executive Family" at Harvard, says that a common attitude among young executives is that if a spouse will only wait until the worker gets settled and earning, there will be time for them later on. Greiff states forcefully, "When a man or woman asks the other to defer life until they make it in the work world—to hang on, things will get better—it assumes that as the man charges forward, his wife will either remain static or develop on her own to his personal satisfaction. It assumes that over a period of time the man will limit and modify his well-established patterns of behavior so as to unite with his growing family. Pure fantasy. It assumes that the rewards of work will justify the neglect of self and family. Equal fantasy. And it assumes that after a number of years in which the family accepts second-best because it has no other choice, the professional can then pick up where he left off.

"In other words, in this situation, the man wants his wife to be independent and dependent in accordance with his career needs and denies her existence as a person who may have her own particular needs. It's a fact that successful families, like successful organizations, require careful thought and planning and persistent attention."[6]

We have long recognized the stresses brought on by work of the father, but we are just beginning to address the additional stresses of having two full-time workers in the family. U.S. Bureau of Census data reveal that between 1950 and 1980, participation of women over the age of sixteen in the labor force increased from 34 percent to 52 percent. The percentage of working married women with children under six years of age shot from about 14 percent in 1950 to 47 percent in 1980, while the percentage of working married women with children aged six to seventeen years doubled, from 33 percent to 64 percent.

Dr. Stephen A. Timm names three critical but surmountable challenges that dual-paycheck couples face: (1) resolving feelings of guilt about working; (2) devoting quality time to both caregiving and career building while still finding time for recreation, community involvement, social relationships, and routine maintenance activities; and (3) arranging for child care.[7]

My research agrees that these, indeed, are the primary stresses brought about by two parents working. Because I will deal with guilt in the following chapter, I want to focus on the second challenge named by Dr. Timm and my respondents: devoting quality time to both family and career plus a plethora of other activities.

Basic to any discussion of this issue is how devoted each parent is to work and to family. When work becomes the primary focus of either spouse's life, the couple relationship is apt to be neglected. In *American Couples,* the authors talk of some men and women who are "relationship-centered" while others put their physical and emotional energies into work. "We call this latter group 'work-centered' although this term includes additional commitments, such as charitable works or an all-consuming hobby. . . . Why do we make these distinctions? We believe that putting one's work first or putting one's partner first has a lot to do with the way a couple functions."

They explain further, "We proceed from the assumption that few people intentionally structure their lives so that their relationship receives less attention than their work. But work sometimes takes over. . . . A traditional husband can pay less attention to the relationship because he knows he can rely on his wife to tend to the couple's emotional life. She is expected to be relationship-centered. Modern two-paycheck couples, married or not, have a dilemma. Neither partner may have time to take care of the relationship."[8]

Even in the traditional marriage with a full-time wife at home, which now represents only 13 percent of our families, I found that when a man is wed to his work, his wife's relationship needs go unmet.

Some spouses have jobs that are less emotionally, but more physically, demanding, like construction work or automotive repair. These are usually nine to five jobs that the worker is able to leave at the workplace, so the spouse or family is not competing with the job for attention at home. But these workers often require more rest because of the physical demands of the job. Their families complain that the worker spends all his time napping after work and on weekends and so is unavailable to spend time with them. Whether the job assumes emotional or physical primacy, then, time pressures remain.

Successful couples and families work very hard to control the encroachment of work into family life. They call each other's attention to neglect of family and demand their right to the worker's presence. One wife said, "Tom's boss would take every minute of his time if I didn't assert our rights to him as a husband and father. When he starts leaving early for breakfast meetings and staying on for dinner meetings, I say, 'Enough, already. You aren't married to the company and you have a family that likes to have you around.'"

A husband shared that he resented his teacher-wife coming home drained at the end of a school day and then spending the evening going over papers and lesson plans. "I suppose I was just one more stress to her because I got on her back, but she is so conscientious that she would spend all her free time on her classes," he said. It took open feelings and attention, but they worked out a satisfactory compromise in which she does paper work some, but not all, evenings now.

An income tax accountant who is basically unavailable to his family from January 1 through April 15 makes up for this lost time and attention by taking off at 3:00 P.M. instead of 5:00 P.M. the rest of the year. He's thus able to greet his kids when they come home from school, a particularly gratifying time for all. "It was either that or get into another line of work," he said. "I found that my wife and kids don't mind my three-and-a-half months away from them as long as they know I care enough about them to give up some time and money to spend with them the rest of the year. They're wonderful about it. At first, my partner was skeptical but I notice he's starting to go home earlier, too."

It's this kind of attention that stress-effective families pay to the role of work in their lives. But doing this goes against a cultural grain that prizes the work ethic and successful worker over the successful parent or spouse. Spouses who demand family time often feel guilty for not wholeheartedly supporting their partner's work or company.

Part of the problem with time lies in our excess of options today. While choices *are* complex, they do offer couples options in dealing with the dilemma of work time versus family time. Stress-reduced families tend to exercise some of these options:

- refusing promotions that require more time away from family
- working less than the proscribed forty hours weekly
- arranging time off in the middle of the week
- refusing to bring extra work home or to work weekends
- turning down promotions requiring a move
- sharing a job with a spouse or co-worker
- trading a raise for more job-hour flexibility
- working at home part of the time
- moving, to cut down commuting time
- asking employers to support on-site day care
- saying no to employers when work interferes with special family times

Some even change jobs that are beginning to affect their marriage and family life, a solution unconsidered in an earlier era. "It just wasn't worth it" is a phrase I heard many times from couples who sacrificed job success for family success.

Older retired parents are the best testifiers to this. When they look back at their lives, they often regret the primacy they put on their work over the emphasis they put on each other. Many admit that if they had it to do over again, they would value family time over work time because family ties and the satisfaction associated with family endure longer than work satisfaction and prestige. Younger couples, especially those who are stress-effective, are beginning to listen to those parents and really hear them.

As more workers show signs of putting marriage and family ahead of job, job performance is beginning to be affected. In *The New Relationships* editorial, we read, "According to recent surveys, the most important issues in America today are love and work—in that order. Are we changing from a work-oriented to a relationship-oriented society? Many employers think so. They complain that the current work force is unproductive, hard to motivate, and unambitious compared to previous generations. Employees refuse to work extra hours, resist relocating, and jump off the fast track before they reach the top of their fields. Workers, themselves, report that family life or time for personal growth is more important to them than their jobs."

The same publication noted that in 1984, for example, six governors decided not to run for the Senate, the next step up the usual political ladder. Political Director Anne Lewis attributes this decision to politicians' undergoing a fundamental shift, like the country in general. "There is increasing interest in private time and family life," she said.[9]

3. Stress-effective couples pay attention to the need for balancing couple time and personal time.

Couple time

Because over half the married men and women respondents chose insufficient couple time as a top stress (for men it is second only to finances and for women, third after finances and lack of shared responsibility in the home), we must examine closely the roadblocks to couple time and the skills some couples use to combat this stress effectively.

Work—the familiar culprit—tops the list of factors. The authors of *American Couples* surveyed respondents on how they deal with the stress that arises when work intrudes into the relationship. They discovered that couples reduce the bickering over the man's job in a number of ways. "When a woman knows that her partner genuinely values time with her, she is less upset about his work because she takes comfort in the assurance that he would be with her if he could," they write. "But when a man says, 'It is important that our relationship does not interfere with other important parts of my life,' . . . a woman may feel that he is intentionally denying her companionship."[10]

Commitment and intimacy are linked. If either a husband's or wife's primary commitment is to work, then their marital intimacy suffers. Time for each other is secondary to time for work or for unwinding from work. Friendship between them begins to diminish. They no longer share deep feelings because doing so would require time and commitment. They eventually become roommates or strangers who simply live together rather than intimates who are willing to become vulnerable by sharing their deepest feelings. Men, especially, are reluctant to take this risk.

In a *McCall's* article, Dianne Hales begins, "He comes home exhausted from a day of too many people and too many problems. All he wants when he walks through the door is less: less talk, less aggravation, less pressure. She's also weary after a day of work or children. But after the final chore she wants something more: more conversation, more companionship, more cuddling. To him, it seems like too much to ask, and he slumps deeper before the television set. She nags. He pours himself another drink and hides behind the newspaper. She cries. He retreats into sullen silence. She attacks ever more fiercely. Eventually the battle becomes full-scale war."[11]

I showed the Hales paragraph to couples when I interviewed them and invited them to respond to it. To a couple, they acknowledged the situation, but stress-effective couples found ways of dealing with it, many of them creative and worth sharing.

I particularly recall a forty-year-old husband's response. He read the paragraph twice, carefully and slowly. Then he said, "That was me, exactly. It's sad . . . so sad." He paused. "But it doesn't have to be that way."

How, I asked, were they able to change? "Simple," he replied. "You choose a wife who says, 'I didn't get married to live alone. Either we're a couple or we're not. You decide and I'll help.'"

He, like so many others, was forced to face the fact that he was giving her and the children his leftover time and it wasn't enough for them. They needed more. She suggested a Marriage Encounter, and he agreed to do it. It turned their marriage around. She learned to back off, and he learned to make connections with her, not just on a few abandoned weekends sprinkled throughout the year, but on a daily basis. Resentment changed to understanding on both parts.

Wayne Rickerson, author of *We Never Have Time Just for Us*, feels that recognition of neglect is crucial to any remedy in a suffering couple relationship. "We do not go into marriage thinking, 'Now our plan is to have fun and excitement, share goals and interests for the first two years, and then neglect these areas.' But we invite neglect into our marriage when we do not *plan* ways to have fun and excitement, share interests, and set common goals."[12]

Planning is fundamental to establishing ongoing quality couple time together, I have found. Couples who really desire more time together make more time available to them to be together. They meet for lunch. They call each other during the day or leave notes to touch base on both important and unimportant matters. They set aside a time of day "just for us." Sometimes it's a jog at 6:00 A.M. or a walk at 10:00 P.M. They guard weekend time and often turn down invitations because they value time alone together.

They develop mutual interests, like the couple I met who make a day of cooking together on Sunday. Or they get excited about a sport and enjoy playing or watching it together. Or they take up a hobby together.

Or they develop a spiritual interest, like studying the Bible. Or they become involved in social action. Or they read to each other so they can share their reactions. Or they enjoy the same soaps and talk about what they would do if they were writing the scripts. Or they take off on unplanned camping trips, just the two of them. (I found spontaneity a hallmark of these couples. When they find themselves with a bonus of extra time due to a blizzard, plant shutdown, or appointment cancellation, they grab the opportunity to do something together, as contrasted with the family that simply turns on the television set.) Or they just relax together in the backyard with the understanding that being together is enough.

The creative possibilities are endless. And the couples who take advantage of them do so because they are willing to say to the world, to their children, and to themselves, "This is the most important person in my life, and I enjoy being with him or her."

This is an enviable dream for many couples, but it wouldn't have to be if they would take the steps to achieve it. Most couples enjoyed each other at one time; after all, that's what brought them together. But when they stop allocating time and energy for each other, enjoyment diminishes. Often a wife takes on the responsibility of rediscovering couple intimacy because she feels the loss more than her husband, but just as often he thwarts her plans or goes along with them begrudgingly, telling her plainly that their relationship is not that important to him. In other couples, the husband recognizes relationship neglect, while the wife is too involved with family, work, or personal interests to really care about remedying it.

But couples who really care use creative remedies. A man wrote to *Woman's Day*, "As my wife works in the morning and I in the evening, I've found that a little extra something I can do for her is drive her to and from work. It saves parking costs and she appreciates my effort. The drive to work gives us precious extra time for sharing, and during the drive home, I am glad to serve as a sympathetic listener for the events of her day. It spares her the bother of fighting traffic and allows her to unwind with the man who was lucky enough to marry her."[13]

Another husband wrote to the same magazine, "Every Wednesday night my wife and I continue a tradition we started in college: We try different wines and cheeses, listen to music, and just talk. The telephone gets unplugged, and no matter what needs to be done, it's put aside. We really listen to each other and have learned a lot. And it's nice to look forward to something in the middle of the week."[14]

Along with having fun together, family therapist Martin Olsen believes that spirituality and sex are two other fundamental areas that couples must pay attention to for a relationship to stay alive. Many couples question the need for shared spirituality, but Olsen explains, "Sharing spiritual experiences . . . not only leads to intimacy but also lifts us out of the humdrum and often materialistic work world. Spiritual sharing need not be limited to discussing God or religion or going to church together. It extends to such existential moments as experiencing favorite music together, discussing literature, enjoying sunsets, appreciating children's laughter, or even struggling with sickness. Spiritual moments are not necessarily pleasant, but if shared openly, they can bring a couple closer."[15]

Time magazine recounts the story of one man who was studied for stress. "While surveying unemployed workers in the Detroit area, University of Michigan researcher Louis Ferman found one hard-luck victim who had been successively laid off by the Studebaker Corp. in 1962 when it was about to fold, a truck manufacturer that went under in the 1970s, and more recently during cutbacks at a Chrysler plant. By all accounts, 'he should have been a basket case,' says Ferman, 'yet he was one of the best-adjusted fellows I've run into.' Asked his secret, the man replied, 'I've got a loving wife and go to church every Sunday.'"[16]

His words echo what I found among family-related professionals who chose "a shared religious core" as one of the traits they most commonly find in families they consider healthy. Many of the healthy families I studied did not have a close church affiliation, but they did have a shared belief that gave meaning and purpose to their lives. Families and couples who do not share a meaning to life or a God tend to become hedonistic, searching for meaning in the "good life." They believe they will be happy and fulfilled if they have their dream home, status, job prestige, and an accumulation of material things. Achieving this goal means putting a premium on work, which often leads to neglect of each other and family. The sad irony, of course, is that when they do achieve the so-called good life, if they do, they have lost the relationships that give life meaning.

That's why we constantly witness the phenomenon of highly successful executives, entertainment figures, and politicians who speak of having their lives turned around when they discover God or yoga or Allah. The rat race, which they have begun to question, becomes less important to them because they have found a deeper meaning to life which, in turn, enriches their personal, couple, and family lives.[7]

Probably the single most obvious and successful example of enriching couple life by adding a spiritual dimension is the Marriage Encounter movement, which combines couple communication and a shared spirituality. Thousands of couples of all, or even no, specific faiths have experienced new life in their marriages as a result of making a Marriage Encounter. The movement, which began as a Roman Catholic effort, has now spread to most other religious denominations.

But the Marriage Encounter doesn't appeal to all. What about the couple who want to add a spiritual intimacy to their union but do not feel attracted to the encounter experience? Some find great satisfaction in joining social action movements like soup kitchens, world relief, peace groups, and the like. Others turn to community or church service which involves giving a deeper part of themselves to serving others. When they do this as a couple, their relationship deepens accordingly.

A couple's sexual life, the third area mentioned by Martin Olsen, can easily suffer when time pressures put stress on a relationship. When one or both are emotionally and physically fatigued from work and excessive activities, sex can become perfunctory, or even absent, instead of exciting, intimate, and renewing. One wife confided, "It's become a chore, like something final to cross off my list of things to do for the day. By the time we go to bed, I'm just too tired to work up any enthusiasm for sex." When a spouse receives no intimacy or attention prior to bedtime, not surprisingly, he or she will resent the request for sexual intercourse. This resentment can be perceived by the partner as disinterest in sex, and he or she will often react with equal resentment. The stress level, then, can become enormous over this issue of sexual and nonsexual intimacy.

In *American Couples,* the authors found, "When the non-sexual parts of couples' lives are going badly their sex life suffers. An unhappy sex life does not necessarily mean that couple is sexually incompatible. Their sexual relationship may be undermined by other problems. Heterosexual couples who say they fight a lot about things like housekeeping, income, expenditures, and whether or not both partners should work are less happy with their sexual relationship. It does not matter what couples fight about," they hold. "Any argument can sour the sexual atmosphere, at least temporarily."[18]

Much more is involved in the sexual relationship than just time, I realize, but time is such a significant factor that it squeezes out other sexual needs, like daytime intimacy. Dr. Olsen tells us, "Couples can work towards intimacy through sex. Though unsatisfactory sex may increase stress in a dual-career marriage, a healthy respect for and enjoyment of each other's sexuality adds a dimension of inner security and a sense of belonging."

He adds, "Distinguishing sexuality from sex is like saying the whole is greater than the sum of the parts. Sexuality includes a self-concept which says, 'I am OK as a total person. I am worthwhile, loving, and lovable.' When a husband assures his wife verbally and non-verbally that she is 'number one' in his life, she has a sense of well-being and an affirmed sexuality that can reduce stress and put that special meaning back into their marriage."[19]

Good sex, like good friendship, demands good time, not just leftover, end-of-the-day time. A leisurely walk after dinner in which couples really talk and listen might be the most effective foreplay possible, in spite of all the sex manuals to the contrary. "Friendship in marriage flourishes in conversations with elbows planted on the table, in contented arguments on the way home about just what was wrong with the movie, in adventures mutually undertaken," say the authors of *Giving Time a Chance: The Secret of a Lasting Marriage.* "A friend is somebody you like spending time with simply because you enjoy being together, and successful long-term marriages hang together for that reason. Each husband and wife have their own definition of what makes up their particular friendship, but many agree that if love is the basis of a thriving marriage, friendship is what makes it work."[20]

Being met occasionally for a shared lunch in a park near work clearly tells a spouse that he or she is enjoyed over fellow workers. I know a teacher-husband whose wife and preschoolers do this a couple of times weekly. "It's just great to drive up to the park and see them there," he said. "I'm with kids and other teachers all day but just 45 minutes with Jenny and the kids sets me up for the rest of the day. I can't tell you what a good feeling it is to get out of the car and have my three-year-old run toward me shouting, 'Daddy, Daddy.'"

He doesn't have to tell us. We all know that feeling if we're lucky. How different from the man who complained that his family didn't care enough to notice when he got home. "I can be home an hour," he said, "and the phone rings and one of the kids asks my wife if I'm home."

Dr. Wayne Oates, professor of psychiatry and author of *When You Can't Find Time for Each Other,* talks about bedtime for couples, a sexually-related stress found in many marriages. "An ungleaned corner of time between husband and wife is often apparent at bedtime. In many instances, one spouse is accustomed to going to bed early; the other prefers to stay up late. Many hesitate to say anything to each other about this. They suffer in silence. They wonder why their mate does not go to bed at the same time as they do. This is especially significant for the sexual life of a couple. This pattern can develop into a power struggle that short-circuits sexual communion. A frank discussion of the time of going to bed, a joint commitment to use this time together creatively with understanding and considerateness increases the quality of the time together. Giving each other your undivided attention at this critical moment each day can improve life at all other points."[21]

Insufficient couple time was mentioned most frequently as a time stress in today's families. If couples pay attention to this time priority, other time-related stresses will be alleviated somewhat. When they have fun, friendship, and good sex together, other stresses diminish. But it takes time.

Personal or "me" time

"Whenever I start to feel stressed I like to work in the garden," a husband told me. "I can get away by myself and really enjoy digging in the dirt. Sometimes when I'm bothered by work worries, my wife says, 'Why don't you go out and work in your roses for awhile?' I really appreciate it when she says that."

His is a familiar way of dealing with stress in healthy families. I found an attitude in healthy families that says an individual has a right to personal time, space, activities, and friends. In stressed families, however, personal time is not regarded as a right as much as a privilege. Children, particularly, have to beg for time of their own in these families. It's as if the family owns the individual's time and doles it out as the family sees fit.

Part of the difficulty in creating "me" time lies in our Puritan heritage, which says that we shouldn't play until our work is done. The reality, of course, is that our work is never going to be done, and if we postpone those activities and friends who refresh and renew us, we will find ourselves on a stressful treadmill with nothing pleasurable to anticipate. Our personal time becomes work time, family time, housekeeping time, couple time, and volunteer time. We begin to wonder what life is all about, if what we are doing is worth the trouble, if it's fair to be expected to give, give, give of ourselves and ask nothing in return. This attitude leads to modern-day martyrdom, and martyrs aren't much fun to live with in the family.

Thousands of people in our culture have sacrificed their personal selves to others' needs *as they viewed them*. They don't want to be accused of being selfish, so although they desperately want more time for themselves, they won't take it. They don't want to be numbered as members of the "me" generation, although they need "me" time.

Stress-reduced families allocate unaccounted-for time to parents and children alike. They recognize the need for one to be alone, to be away from the rest of the family at times, to stop what he or she is doing when the stress level gets high and to have some fun. The healthy parent will stop in the middle of housecleaning and read a story. The healthy spouse will tell his or her partner to go out and smell the roses for awhile. The children of healthy parents do not demand all the parents' time as theirs but enjoy having parents who can enjoy themselves.

The need to be alone at times is very strong for all of us. I have found that when my adolescent sons go through perfectly normal periods of moody withdrawal from the family, the best antidote is to get them to the lake, mountains, or farmland, where they can roam, fish, hike, and get away by themselves. An afternoon alone with nature sets them up for another month of living with the family. The same thing is true of their parents, I might add.

In their research for *American Couples,* authors Schwartz and Blumstein asked couples about personal time. "We found that on average women need more private time than men. Since women are in general more relationship-centered than men, we were surprised by this result," they said. "It told us that even though women center their lives around their relationships, they feel a great need to get away occasionally to pursue personal interests. These may include spending time with friends, attending to one's parents or other relatives, taking care of household business, spending time at a hobby, or simply relaxing."[22]

Most couples I interviewed who make room for "me" time steer away from activities that require a lot of planning, equipment, money, and companions, preferring simpler relaxation.

4. Stress-effective people recognize their own stress level and take early steps to counter it.

I found these adults to be finely tuned in to their own stress levels, in contrast to others who don't recognize or acknowledge a stress until it becomes overwhelming. At the extreme, the latter are the ones who erupt in violence after keeping a tight lid on their daily stresses rather than dealing with them at the time. In 1983 I was asked to testify at the Attorney General's Task Force on Domestic Violence about what happens in healthy families that prevents violent reactions to stress. My response then and now is that violence is much less likely if people *recognize stresses early.*

Individuals who recognize their own stress symptoms aren't just lucky or clairvoyant but have learned (often through unpleasant experience) their own signs of distress. "I know that when I start feeling sorry for myself I need some time for me," one mom told me. "If I try to wish it away, it just gets worse and I say hateful things to my children and husband."

"I start to eat," said another. "I eat everything in sight, even things I don't usually like. That's a sign that I need to get outside and do something that's fun. Usually I call a friend and we play tennis."

A husband told me he gets away from family and co-workers. "I just don't want to deal with them when I begin to feel really stressful. I resent having to answer their questions or talk on the phone. If I don't get away at that point and spend some badly needed time alone I find myself disliking them intensely."

We all have different stress levels and symptoms. Those who deal with stress most effectively are those who best recognize their own stress level, pinpoint symptoms, and take steps to reduce it. What are these steps? I found six most often used by stress-reduced respondents.

They participate in physical activities. Not only do they jog, exercise, walk, play tennis or golf, but also they use stress-relieving techniques like deep breathing, yoga, stretching, and other relaxation methods. I was struck by the number of people in healthy families who choose first a physical activity when they feel their stress level rising. Many like to get out in the yard and do hard physical labor. Some straighten their garages, and some begin to clean closets or basements with a vengeance. "Just watch out when I reach that stage," one wife said. "I will throw anything out." I can respond to her. It's a wonderful time to get rid of clutter.

In *Kicking Your Stress Habits,* psychologist and author Donald A. Tubesing tells readers to "listen to your body. It will let you know when you are pushing too hard. When the back or head aches or stomach sours, slow down, have some fun, take the time to enjoy the world around you. Set aside some time each day for self-indulgence. Focus on life's little pleasures." And he emphasizes, "Revitalize through exercise. A body lacking in physical stamina is in no shape to handle stress. An exercise tuneup can increase your emotional as well as your physical strength. Exercise enhances, rather than saps, your energy; it also has a distinct relaxing effect."[23]

They believe that a change in routine is as good as a rest. These families search for ways to vary their routine at work or in the home. They change work habits, breaking up work with relaxation or pleasure. They may get a part-time job if they don't work, or they may change jobs if they feel their work is becoming too stressful. They focus on what they have accomplished more than what they haven't. They let some things go. They look at their volunteer work and ask themselves, "Is this really enjoyable or is it too much like work?" One woman who had been active in the League of Women Voters took a sabbatical from it when it became routine and volunteered with a Meals on Wheels program for a year, instead. "When I went back to League, I really enjoyed it but I had become tired with it after five years," she said.

Dr. Tubesing suggests, "Get outside yourself. Stress causes people to turn into themselves and focus too much on their own problems. Try doing something for someone else. Or find something other than yourself and your accomplishments to care about. Be more tolerant and forgiving of yourself and others."[24]

They share dreams, expectations, and disappointments more readily than other families. When they feel their stress level escalating, these family members are able to say, "Hey, look, I'm important and I'm unhappy. I need some help around here." They don't depend on an occasional blowup to change family patterns but voice needs and issues before they reach the explosion point. One woman shared a common frustration over the summer return of college students. "They became accustomed to picking up a tray of food at the college cafeteria and then putting the dirty dishes on the conveyor belt. When they came home, there wasn't any conveyor belt so they left their dirty dishes on the counter waiting for me to rinse them and put them in the dishwasher. After a week of this, I said, 'Okay, gang, do I look like a conveyor belt? I don't see myself that way and you're not going to, either. How do we solve this problem?' They weren't even aware of it. I gave them a choice of doing their own rinsing or living with an angry nag. They chose the rinsing."

A dad shared the frustration of being responsible for putting gas in the cars. "For a long time I just did it rather than create a scene but finally I said to my teenage drivers, 'Anybody old enough and smart enough to drive is old enough and smart enough to put gas in the car. If you want to use the car, I expect you to keep it clean and gassed up.'"

In instances like these, the parent is saying, "I have needs and stresses and I expect you to help with them." This is in distinct contrast to the parent who keeps serving while boiling inside—a direct route to stress and parent burnout.

They re-evaluate their recreational activities. These families ask themselves, Are we really enjoying our recreation or are we doing it because others like it? At a family stress workshop near the Rocky Mountains, I found recreation to be an area that really causes conflict. Many of these participants admitted that they didn't particularly like to ski but went because the family enjoyed it. "Skiing takes so much preparation that it's no fun for me," said one mother. "By the time I search out the proper clothing, get the tickets, prepare lunches and snacks for all of us, and run herd on the kids and their equipment, I'm too pooped to have fun. Actually, I don't even like to ski but I go because it's a family outing."

"What would you like to do instead?" I asked.

"I would like for them to go skiing and for me to be alone at home with a good book," she said.

I find that many parents share her feelings. They plan recreation around what the kids enjoy rather than what they enjoy. Some of this is inevitable, of course, but stress-reduced parents also find time for activities they enjoy.

They spend time with friends. Good friends are one of the best outlets for sharing feelings, laughter, and enjoyment when stress becomes high. Yet friends are one of the first groups to go when time becomes precious. In *American Couples,* the authors talk about the varying need for friends among couples. "Just as some people feel left out of their partner's leisure activities with other friends, some feel deprived simply by their partner's need for solitude. If they themselves rarely experience such a need, they may feel rejection when their partner prefers to be alone. . . . Although it is common for men to want a 'night out with the boys,' and women to want 'time with their girl friends,' some people still worry that their partner's need to be with friends (of the same sex) really reflects flight from the relationship."[25]

Even when partners encourage the other to develop special friends, it isn't always that simple. In "I'm Lonely," Susan Jacoby writes, "My friend Elizabeth is lonely in an entirely different way. She has a devoted husband, a two-year-old daughter and a demanding job. . . . How could a woman with such a full life possibly be lonely? 'Except for my husband,' she says, 'I hardly ever talk to anyone my own age. I can't go out with my colleagues for a drink on the way home from school; I can't go out shopping with a friend on Saturday. There isn't enough of me to go around for friends any more. My life is a shuttle between my classroom and my baby at home.'"[26]

While her situation is by no means rare, I found it less common among healthy couples. Instead, they encourage one another to spend some time with friends. Why not stop for a drink with friends on the way home? That half hour might well enhance your family time at home. The value of friends, according to stress authorities, is that they listen when we need to vent. "Talk it out," encourages Dr. Tubesing. "Problems often seem much worse when you alone carry their burden. Talking to a trusted friend or relative, or a professional counselor, can help you sort things out and unload some of the burden. If things are really bad, don't hesitate to seek professional counseling or psychotherapy."[27] Paradoxically, many therapists claim that their clients wouldn't really need them if they had kept their friendships in order. It's when they have let their friends drop and have nobody with whom to share daily worries and dreams that they must turn to professional help.

Single parents, who suffer most from lack of personal time, need close friends more than other parents. Yet, in their struggle to be sole parent and provider, they find little time for themselves and for friends. One mother of two who suffered occasional bouts of depression solved her problem by redeveloping friendships. "I learned in a most painful way that friends are not a luxury but a necessity for good mental health," she said.

They nurture their spiritual life. Meditation, reflection, spirituality, are areas often neglected by people who are caught on the fast track. They simply don't take time to reflect upon meaning in life because they are so caught up in catching up. In recent years we have seen renewed interest in meditative techniques. Many healthy people admit to meditating and praying in an informal way and in some strange places: in the car, while walking or running, on a commuter train, or during a boring meeting. Several told me that they would not want to give up their car commute because this is the only time they can be alone to think about deeper issues and to talk with God. When I was lecturing in Santa Clara and planning on taking a train into San Francisco at the end of the day, a counselor offered to drive me instead. I demurred because he had already had a full day and it was a ninety-minute drive each way. "I need some prayer and reflection time," he said, "and I find it much easier to do that in the car than on my knees."

Some people find poetry or music ideal for stress reduction, and others find Scripture or other spiritual reading relaxing and encouraging. But whatever one uses, developing this deeper dimension of ourselves is undeniably conducive to a more harmonious relationship with our world and the people in it. Many highly stressed adults have found profound release by focusing, occasionally, on matters of the soul instead of always on the humdrum of daily life.

I frequently go to El Pomar, a renewal center at the base of Pike's Peak, to write, and while there recently, I counted seven adults taking advantage of what the Center calls A Day Away. For a small fee, people can spend the day in a peaceful and pastoral setting, roam at will, visit the library, nap, read, swim. "I come here about twice a month to recharge my batteries," an oncology nurse told me. "I work with dying patients and their families and that could lead to despair if I let it. This is the best bargain in mental health anywhere around."

5. Stress-reduced families play together.
Next to my son who was born on Mother's Day, the best Mother's Day gift I ever received was the game of Trivial Pursuit this past year. We have never been much of a game-playing family, but this game has given us much pleasure and many laughs as a family. "Gee, Dad," one of the kids quipped, "I didn't know you knew so much junk."

As we sat playing on into the wee hours the other night, I realized anew the relationship between family enjoyment and family bonding. There's something about playing and laughing together that says to a family, "We're a unit. We share a history and a future. We have to work and live together, but we also enjoy having fun together."

Virginia Satir, one of our most respected family scholars, says that families are so busy they end up with half-contacts with each other and don't have time to build a family identity. After studying stress-effective families, I submit that part of the reason for this is time, but another part is the inability to have fun together.

Some families ignore playtime for a variety of reasons: they develop an attitude that fun is peer-oriented and individualistic; their schedules are so full that family fun-time gets squeezed out; they lack spontaneity and come to believe that family recreation requires planning, equipment, and money, which may be in short supply; or they rely upon television as their sole recreational activity. Other families defer fun together until their annual vacation. Finally, and sadly, some families simply do not enjoy one another.

Playing together as a family sounds almost too simple, but it is a major factor in living with stress in the modern family. Many families spend a great deal of time together in child-related activities like league sports and scouting, but they don't play together as a family. I found that the families with the most ability to deal with everyday family tension are those who recognize the need to temper work and activities with shared play. "When tempers get short and tensions get high because we are so busy and pressured for time, we know we need to stop and have some fun," said a father.

And how do families have fun? Following is a list of activities families mentioned. Some will come as a surprise to other families who don't view "raking leaves" as fun, but the family who submitted it does. They built a tradition around raking the leaves in the fall and having a leaf-fueled wiener-and-marshmallow roast. At last count, one teen told me, they accumulated twenty-eight family friends to rake, play, laugh, and eat together. In short, this family makes fun and creates bondedness out of what other families might perceive as work.

I present this list to families with the suggestion that they mark the activities they enjoy doing together and then, individually, prioritize them in order of enjoyment, adding others that are not on the list. Some families will *never* want to shop together, but others enjoy it a lot. Some will love porch or patio chatting, while others wonder why. Since families are unique, it's helpful to name activities special to each.

Finally, I suggest families post the activities named collectively as most enjoyable and do a weekly or monthly audit, asking, "Have we had fun together lately?" If the answer is no, the stress level is apt to be high, and it's a cue to families to find time for playing together.

FAMILY PLAY ACTIVITIES

- Volleyball
- Fishing
- Camping
- Hiking
- Biking
- Playing cards: which games?
- Swimming
- Watching a sports activity: which?
- Telling stories
- Reading aloud
- Playing board games: which?
- Sitting and talking
- Watching TV: which programs?
- Playing softball
- Sailing
- Canoeing
- Playing croquet
- Cooking: what?
- Shopping: where?
- Visiting: whom?
- Driving: where?
- Skiing: where?
- Going to the beach: where?
- Movies: what kind?
- Dancing: where?
- Eating out: where?
- Praying: reading Scripture
- Singing: what?
- Outdoor concerts
- Family parties: which ones?
- Wrestling on the floor
- Going to a cabin
- Going to the circus
- Fixing/washing cars

- Telling jokes
- Garage sales
- Gardening
- Cleaning the garage
- Sewing
- Doing crafts or models together
- Playing with electric train
- Painting the house
- Raking leaves
- Christmas caroling
- Making Christmas gifts/cookies
- Decorating the tree
- Taking care of pets
- Going to the zoo
- Going to museums/planetarium
- Parades
- Craft fairs
- Church bazaars
- Carnivals and fairs
- Golfing
- Looking at colleges
- High school plays
- Dinner theaters
- Jigsaw puzzles
- Building something
- Collecting: what?
- Kick-the-can
- Playing catch
- Bingo
- Family birthdays
- Ice-/roller-skating
- Sledding
- Building snowmen
- Crossword puzzles
- Visiting the cemetery
- Playing Twenty Questions
- Taking a walk
- Jogging or running
- Being silly

- Sleeping outside
- Talking politics
- Family retreats
- Family reunions
- Watching Little League games
- Going to high school games
- Going to school concerts
- Playing backgammon or chess
- Easter activities
- Fourth of July picnics
- Family fireworks
- Family skits

These families frequently include other people in their play. This is particularly true of families whose children and adolescents feel free to invite their friends to play with the family, whether it's a Sunday cookout or a game of cards. Many families end up with the children of nonplaying families who enjoy an element missing in their own family life. A common complaint of families is that adolescents do not want to do anything with their families, but I didn't find this true in the healthy families I studied. Rather, families who develop a habit of play often find their adolescents including peers in the activity rather than losing them to a peer activity. I discovered three families who have an annual family New Year's Eve party that they celebrate with two or three other families. As their children grew older, they expected them to want to go to their own peer activities on New Year's Eve, but many expressed the surprise that the teens want to come to their party and bring their friends. Stress-reduced families, then, tend to welcome others into their play activities.

6. Stress-effective families prioritize activities.

An overscheduled calendar was named by 32 percent of married women and 39 percent of married men as one of their top ten family stresses. Only 20 percent of single mothers named it as a stress, and I suspect that their already-dual roles prevent them from filling up the calendar with social and children's activities to the extent that other families do. In modern families, both parents and adolescent children frequently have full- or part-time jobs. When we add to this housekeeping duties and the likelihood that each member will have other activities or meetings, the squeeze for time to relax and play is enormous. The first items to go are couple, personal, and family playtimes. Yet these are the prescriptions most likely to reduce stress in family life.

Learning to prioritize is a feature of the stress-effective family. Parents in these families take the lead by constantly scrutinizing their activities with an eye toward paring them down. They learn to live with lower housekeeping standards. They don't strive to have a perfect lawn. They learn to say no to school, church, and community leaders who ask them to volunteer for activities that will take away from family time. They drop clubs and organizations. They don't feel guilty if they aren't deeply involved in community activities. They feel more confident than other parents in being able to say "No, that's family time" or "I need to spend some time with my wife."

Dr. Stephen A. Timm talks about establishing priorities. "This means deciding each day what the important activities are that you want to get done. The best way to establish priorities is to begin each day with a To Do list. To Do lists can be made separately for home and work. Here are the guidelines: (1) make a new list at the start of each day; (2) have between four and six items; (3) rank the items in the order of importance; (4) complete the items in that order except when an item needs to be completed at a particular time, then go ahead with other items until the designated time."

He stresses the need to block out time in advance for family activities. "Get your calendar and plan activities and time together for the entire year. Make these times sacred and untouchable so that only a visit from the president of the United States might interfere. If you do not plan for time together, you most likely will never get around to it and will be plagued by feelings of guilt over neglecting one another. There is a minimum amount of time that families must spend together to maintain harmony and well-being. That amount varies from family to family, but when a family drops below its minimum, problems appear."[28]

Dr. Tubesing offers a pithy formula for prioritizing: "Divide your tasks into three categories: essential, important and trivial, and forget about the trivial. Hire others, including your own children, to do the tasks that can be farmed out. Learn to say no when you're asked to do something that overloads your time or stress budget or diverts you from what you really consider most important. Be satisfied with a less-than-perfect-job if the alternative is not getting a job done at all. Identify the activities you find satisfying in and of themselves and focus on enjoying the activities themselves, rather than your performance or what rewards they will bring."[29]

In dealing with time pressures, stress-effective families
1. view time as a controllable commodity,
2. balance work and family life,
3. balance couple and personal time,
4. recognize their stress level and take early steps to counter it,
5. play together,
6. prioritize activities.

7

Shared Responsibility, Work, Self-Esteem and . . . Guilt, Guilt, Guilt . . .

Unhappiness with the work situation was named as a top stress by *men* but not by women. *Lack of shared responsibility in the home, housekeeping standards, guilt for not accomplishing more, and self-image/self-esteem/ feelings of unattractiveness* were named as top stresses by *women* but not by men.

* * *

"If the yellow waxy buildup doesn't get you, the guilt will."

—Thirty-year-old wife

Although this chapter may appear to be a catchall, it actually gathers up related stresses which were named among the top ten on either the men's or women's lists but not both. Some can be viewed as the same stress applied to differing lifestyles, that is, unhappiness with the work situation (men) might be expressed by women as lack of housekeeping standards or shared responsibility in the family. And if a woman views her home as her work, or part of her work, it follows that unhappiness with housekeeping standards will increase her guilt and decrease her self-esteem.

These issues are delicately intertwined and exacerbated by the dramatic change in working patterns and husband/wife roles taking place in our culture. *Lack of shared responsibility in the home* was named as second highest of ten stresses by married women and tenth by single mothers, a clear expression of dissatisfaction with the imbalance of household responsibility in a world where over half of these women hold down full-time jobs. "If I can take on a job, you can take on the dishes" is the message these women are giving to their husbands and children. But in stressed families the message isn't getting through, and the imbalance increases resentment, tension, and family stress.

Family scholars, futurists, and sociologists are beginning to recognize and study a major shift in how couples view one another, roles, work, and power, a shift that shows no sign of abating. Some couples react to this shift with great stress, while others are able to use it to advantage in controlling stress.

In *American Couples,* the authors speak of this shift: "A common set of questions and challenges confronts *all* 'types' of couples today. The changing nature of male and female roles creates problems as couples go about even the most mundane tasks. For example: Who should do what within the household? The question is not simply who cooks, who takes out the trash, and who repairs the leaky faucet. Such task arrangements are really only a small part of the division of chores in a partnership. The larger question is much more profound and less amenable to easy answers. The household provides symbolic occasions for the establishment of territory and authority. Couples are trying to grapple with how men and women, how men and men, how women and women should relate to one another. Where is fairness and justice? What is compromise? What is the 'rightful' province of male or female expertise? Whose needs—or perceptions of needs—will guide the relationship?"[1]

These questions underline the stresses named by men and women in this chapter, and upon their answers depends the ability of a family to deal with them well. John Naisbitt, author of *Megatrends,* echoes other futurists when he sees this cultural shift as positive and hopeful. "The eleventh mega-trend is a shift from sex roles to synergy. It reflects a reconciliation between the sexes at a deep level, a greater harmony between qualities we used to consider either masculine or feminine. It could well mean the end of the battle of the sexes," he says. He believes that competition between the sexes has begun to give way to a new kind of cooperation based on individual contribution because men are seeing that the old ways of wielding power cause great stress in their relationships with women.

Couples who experience stress in the relationship between home, work, and each other need to understand just what this shift means. In the past, we had a dependency/independency cultural pattern. Women were dependent, and men were independent—or at least, these were the culturally approved and respected roles. Men worked, women didn't. If women worked, men were employers, women employees. Men made the money and decisions; women made food and clothing. This tidy, unquestioned role pattern was blessed by church and community. Until things began to change . . .

We are now moving rapidly toward a relationship in which we both need each other, in which we are both dependent upon and independent of one another, or interdependent. Naisbitt and others call this mutuality "synergy."

Instead of dividing our lives into spheres—he responsible for financial security and she for emotional security—we are now holding both responsible for each sphere. As this shift escalates, people who rigidify into old dependency/independency roles while trying to live in today's world can experience great stress in dealing with work, household responsibilities, self-esteem, and guilt.

I'm tempted in this chapter to mention superficial solutions that couples work out to deal with this shift—shared grocery shopping, for example—but until the couple understands and addresses the value system out of which they are operating, the solutions will be temporary and the feelings that cause ongoing resentment will not lessen. Rather, they will emerge repeatedly with ever-greater intensity over a myriad of issues. Healthy families display the following characteristics to deal effectively with the stresses covered in this chapter:

- They are embracing a new value system.
- They share responsibilities in the home.
- They live with lower housekeeping standards.
- They empathize with spouse or parents who are unhappy in their jobs.
- They minimize guilt.
- They have good self-esteem.
- They exhibit family bonding and optimism that tells them they can handle any ordinary stress.

1. Healthy families are embracing a new value system.

I found that families most able to deal with role stresses are also most likely to understand and accept the Emerging Value System outlined below, as contrasted with highly-stressed families who rigidly operate within the Traditional Value System. Here are some of the contrasts between the two value systems:

Power

Traditional Value System: "I have the power so I can treat you as I like."
Emerging Value System: "I will be treated with dignity and acceptance regardless of my power."

In family life, the Traditional Value System assumes the breadwinner is the one to be catered to because he or she is more important. This person makes the decisions and treats a spouse and children as unequal persons. But people who are not treated with dignity are leaving marriages today. Children not treated with dignity are leaving home, by court order if they are young, by choice if older. In couples operating under the Emerging Value System, this inequality does not exist. Couples treat each other and children with acceptance and dignity regardless of earning power.

Authority

Traditional Value System: "Society grants me authority because I am man, parent, teacher, clergy, white, or rich."
Emerging Value System: "I am equal and I assume equality even though I may be woman, child, student, lay, black, or poor. I shouldn't have to fight for this equality because it is my right, even though society may try to deny it to me."

In the Traditional Value System, women and children were granted less esteem simply because they were women and children, and consequently, they assumed less self-esteem—at a tremendous cost to both personal and family health. In the Emerging Value System, families grant esteem and equality to members regardless of their age or gender. Boys are not esteemed more than girls. Older children are not esteemed more than younger. One spouse is not esteemed over another, but all are mutually esteemed.

Relationship

Traditional Value System: "There must be one up and one down in any relationship."
Emerging Value System: "We are peers in any good relationship."

In family life, this simply means that everyone is heard, rather than the traditional "Parents know best and children should not be heard" and "Husbands know more than wives, so women shouldn't vote," etc. Decisions are based on the entire family's needs and desires, not on the strongest member's wishes. Consensus is prized more than one-upmanship in these families.

Success

Traditional Value System: "Competition is the highest value in becoming successful. We must compete with one another and teach our children to compete if they are to achieve success."

Emerging Value System: "Cooperation is the highest value in becoming successful. We must learn to negotiate and teach our children to cooperate if they are to be successful."

Tension over competition versus cooperation is evident in many families who struggle with stress. One parent may view competition as a high value, while the other sees it as divisive. One parent may pit siblings against each other, believing this will produce more successful children, while the other perceives it as damaging to their relationship. As I mentioned in the chapter on children, parents who push their children to compete in sports or in activities or for popularity give rise to more stressful children than those who encourage their children to develop noncompetitive skills and relationships.

Intimacy

Traditional Value System: "Intimacy is physical. Sexual attractiveness is most important."
Emerging Value System: "Intimacy is verbal, emotional, and sexual. Can I share feelings as well as physical sex? Sexual attractiveness comes second to emotional attractiveness."

Couples operating in the Traditional Value System put a high priority on their physical attractiveness and lovemaking, while those operating in the Emerging Value System put a deeper value on risking vulnerabilities, on sharing deep emotions, and on appreciating one another for less visible values. Aging, for example, can be highly stressful for the former couples, while it frequently enriches the relationship of the latter.

Roles and Goals

Traditional Value System: "I know what my goals are, and I will assume a role to achieve them."
Emerging Value System: "I know what my role is, and I will assume goals to achieve it."

This shift can be the most difficult to express and understand. In the Traditional Value System, a person said, "I want to make enough money to live the good life with a home, vacations, and security, and I am willing to become someone I don't particularly want to be in order to achieve this. I will take a job I don't like, or I will become a workaholic, or I will go into my father's business to achieve this, even though that's not the kind of person I am."

In the Emerging Value System, people are saying, "I am not cut out for the corporate jungle, for farming, or for full-time homemaking, so I will look for work that suits my needs, even if it pays less." This can be a major source of stress in families where a spouse decides to escape from the Traditional Value System by changing to a job that is more satisfying and less lucrative. It can be even more stressful between generations, especially for parents who do not understand their young adult's decision to accept lower-paying work because it is more personally satisfying. Many parents attribute this to selfishness on the part of the young, while their children in turn charge parents with being interested only in money.

In the Traditional Value System, job success is all important. In the Emerging Value System, work satisfaction is as important as job success.

Decisions

Traditional Value System: "I will make decisions that meet our needs as I perceive them."

Emerging Value System: "What I do affects you and others in my life, so decisions will be made by all of us."

Under the Traditional Value System, a man commonly accepted a move without question and without consulting the family. This doesn't occur in a family operating under the Emerging Value System. Children's needs, a wife's work, happiness with schools, and other issues are considered before a move is made. In the Traditional Value System, economic advantages determined family operations, while in the Emerging Value System, personal issues determine family operations.

In presenting the above, I don't mean to imply that the Emerging Value System is superior to the Traditional Value System but to explain that I found the Emerging Value System operating more frequently in stress-reduced families. Each system has strengths and strains because value systems evolve to meet the cultural needs of a particular era. Judging the merits of either system is not an issue here. However, some individuals, families, and groups feel strongly that the Traditional System is the one to which we should return, and, consequently, they place a moral label on this system, which motivates them to work politically and religiously to restore it. Other groups are equally dedicated to acceptance of the Emerging Value System, so the issue has become politically divisive in both philosophical and geographical areas.

I am not concerned with the politics but with the stresses that occur when value systems collide within a family. After studying the above, it's easy to see why stresses unheard of in earlier families are tearing families apart today. It was easier when men accepted that they would have to work in unpleasant jobs, when women assumed they were solely responsible for home and children, and when children assumed parents were always right because they had the authority. As these families move toward the Emerging Value System, which sociologists call the most profound value shift in relationships in history, stresses are bound to increase unless the couple addresses personal values which have changed, and will continue to change, their relationship in the years ahead. Divorce mediators claim that a great number of divorces that occur among couples married fifteen to twenty-five years stem from an inability of couples to recognize value shifts and move together from one system to the next.

In describing the marriage scene ten years ago, marriage researchers David and Vera Mace agreed that "traditional marriage is an anachronism and will not survive in our new, open society." They believed that the transition from traditional marriage to companionship in marriage involves such a tremendous reversal of values and roles that the majority of American couples have not been able to make the transition:

"They have tried to be companions in marriage and ended up being adversaries," they wrote.

Theirs was a prophetic insight. The stresses of couples detailed in this chapter will illustrate the fallout of moving into a companionship marriage. Younger couples who are marrying today have a better opportunity for establishing compatibility in value and role systems than older couples who began in one system and moved unevenly into another. Social psychologist Zick Rubin says of this group, "Men who came of age in the late 1960s and early 1970s . . . have grown up with new expectations about work and family. These men, many of whom are now in their 30s, are less likely to base their self-esteem solely on their success as breadwinners and more eager to devote time to their families and home life."[2]

In the families I interviewed, I found the least amount of stress among those who were moving together toward the Emerging Value System. However, I also found couples who were both satisfied in the Traditional Value System and not stressed except in the area of children, who tend to operate toward, or in, the Emerging Value System. Then the stresses become enormous. "My husband and I feel that he is the head of the family and that I should stay home and be responsible for the children," said the wife in one of these couples. "We belong to a church that preaches this and we believe it is God's plan for families. But our children don't accept this and we feel as if we have failed as parents."

Children, of course, have always led parents into a new culture, whether it is a physical or value culture. They are leading us into a computer culture through their growing knowledge and ability to use advanced technology, just as the children of immigrants led their parents into the American culture by learning its language and adopting its customs while their parents tried to hang on to their own familiar culture. Children today see nothing unusual about the Emerging Value System because they never experienced the Traditional System in totality. Unlike their parents and grandparents, they never lived under the convenience and comfort of a solid value system which went unquestioned by society. Today's children were born into the midst of a changing value system, and they assume that it's natural to question authority, to share power, to demand to be treated with dignity, and to negotiate for consensus. They assume rights in high school that their parents would never have assumed and expect to be treated with respect by those in authority, whether in the family, school, work, or even the military.

These children can be a notable stress in families whose strong religious orientation is based on the morality of the Traditional Value System, although they live in a world moving toward an Emerging Value System. A religious leader proclaims, "God established that fathers were to preside in the home. A mother's role is also God-ordained. Mothers are to conceive, bear, nourish, love, and train. They are helpmates and counsel with their husbands. There is no inequality between the sexes in God's plan. It is a matter of division of responsibility."

He may speak for God, but not all will agree with him. Whose responsibility is it to bring home the money, to drive children to activities, to help with housework, to deal with financial worries? Since responsibility was named as such a high stress among women, let's examine how the stress-effective family deals with responsibility in the home.

2. Stress-reduced families tend to share responsibility. These families also tend to respect one another's feelings and needs more than those who are stressed by lack of shared responsibility. Instead of a constant battle over who does what or ongoing requests on the part of a parent, these family members assume a responsibility for economizing, for helping with chores, and for supporting one another as a natural part of family life. How do they reach this point?

"It's hard to answer that question," responded one wife. "From the time we were married we pitched in and helped each other, whether it was with housework or outside work. Our kids just followed that example as they grew up. If my husband brings work home in the evening, I don't want to watch television while he's working so I help him with it by typing or whatever. And he never sits and watches television while I'm trying to clean the house. We just all get in and work together on it."

A single parent reported that the family simply divides household tasks evenly and doesn't use a lot of emotional energy refighting chore allocation. "Each of us has a room to keep clean and if it isn't clean, nothing fun like TV or friends can be enjoyed. I cook the dinner but the kids do the after-dinner work. We all fold the laundry and put it away. Sure, we have some arguments but we stay on top of them."

These families don't view mother as maid—a common complaint of highly stressed women. They respect her too much to sit around and let her serve them. It's more a question of respect than responsibility, not "You should do it because you're the mother," but "We share because we care about you."

Husbands in these families don't enjoy living with resentful martyrs, either. "Life is much more pleasant when she's happy," one quipped. "And when she's doing all the work, she's not happy."

And their children are more resourceful. They feel more ownership in the family because they are given more opportunities to be responsible, not just in chore-sharing but in managing their own lives. I recall the time our twelve-year-old son embedded a fishing hook in his finger at a lake about six blocks from the family medical clinic. He clipped the line, walked to the clinic, got two stitches and a tetanus shot, before calling us to come and pick him up.

A friend of mine was astonished at my equanimity. "I would have been furious with my son if he'd done that."

It was my turn to be mystified. "Why?" I asked.

"Because I would want to be with him at the clinic and talk with the doctor. And to walk six blocks with a fishhook in his finger . . ." She shuddered.

I didn't have the courage to tell her that instead of being angry with Steve, we complimented him on handling the situation. He did exactly what an adult would have done. He didn't fall apart at the sight of a fishhook dangling from his finger, and while he was proud of taking care of it, he didn't think it was any "big deal." Now, if I could get him to find the hamper as easily as the clinic. . . .

The critical point in families arises when a mother who has been at home takes an outside job. How the family views her decision is crucial in determining their willingness to absorb some of the chores she had earlier assumed as hers.

Blumstein and Schwartz write, *"Married couples who disagree about the wife's right to work have less happy relationships.* Most working wives do so with the accord of their husbands, and husbands and wives decide together whether the woman will work full time or part time. But when the couple fights about her working, the relationship is strained. Sometimes the fights stem from the husband's reaction to the effect the wife's full time work has on the household. He considers the household to be her responsibility and is angry about her absence."[3]

They also found that even when wives have full-time jobs, they continue to do most of the housework, with only 22 percent of husbands, as compared with 59 percent of wives, performing at least eleven hours of housework each week. Many husbands of working wives felt strongly opposed to doing housework and resentful when they had to.

"When husbands do a lot of housework, married couples have greater conflict," they state emphatically. "Married men's aversion to housework is so intense it can sour their relationship. The more housework they do, for whatever reason, the more they fight about it. If this pattern continues into the future, it will be a major barrier to the reorganization of husbands' and wives' roles. One husband in his early forties described his feelings about housework: 'We have a very traditional labor pattern. Very traditional. She does all the household chores—at least up to a short time ago. Then all I did was take out the garbage. . . . Now she's at work and I have to help out more, but I resist doing things I'm not supposed to do. I'll do the outside work, but the inside work has always been her territory and I don't think I should have to learn things that she has spent twenty years perfecting. . . . So we have got me in this mode of helper—which I don't like very much—but it is more necessary right now if

the house is going to be well kept. . . . I am willing to make her life a little easier but I can't say I enjoy any of it.'"⁴

Women tend to react to this kind of statement with guilt or anger or both. "Nobody ever asked me if *I* enjoyed it," one woman said after hearing this man's quote. "Let's face it, housework is unpleasant and his wife attended to that unpleasantness for twenty years. I really can't empathize with him at all."

Another said he reminded her not only of her own husband but of her children as well. "They make me feel guilty if I ask them to help. I don't particularly like my job but we need the money and still they act as if they're doing me a favor by letting me work. I vacillate between guilt and anger."

Blumstein and Schwartz observe, "When the husband was making the only money the couple had, it was traditional for the wife to make his life at home as comfortable as possible. Since his labor was synonymous with the couple's welfare, doing things for him was doing something for the whole family. Men learned to be indulged without feeling particularly selfish. . . . They became accustomed to doing no housework unless they wished to be magnanimous, and . . . it is still difficult for men to give up these privileges."⁵

Men in stress-reduced families give up these privileges more quickly than others, I found, although they don't like doing chores any more than their wives or children do. One interesting observation I had is that when Dad helps, the kids tend to help more agreeably. When Dad doesn't help, Mom has more struggles in getting the children to share in household responsibilities.

On a positive note, Blumstein and Schwartz found that the happier employed wives are with their jobs, the happier they are in their marriage. "We believe that when they work—and enjoy it—they indeed satisfy many of their needs," the authors say. "Consequently they can place fewer demands on their husband and are more content with their marriage."⁶

So, the good news is that if a wife enjoys her work outside the home, it can lead to a better relationship with her husband, which could offset stress arising from lack of shared responsibility in the home.

This improved relationship may stem from men and women experiencing each other's roles for the first time. According to Herbert Hendin, "The discontent of women with children and of men with work, the sexual war that ensues when each sex imagines the other has it easier, have led many people to seek a coalescence of opportunities, responsibilities, and experiences between men and women. As women are accepted into business, the academy, and the profession as equal competitors, many are becoming aware of the pressures that men confront and the limitations there can be on a career. As men become more involved with young children, some begin to understand the intense emotional demands children make on women."[7] This shared experience led one family researcher to conclude that instead of viewing their career as work or family, we should encourage families to view *the integration of work and family* as their career.

Single mothers, while expecting and receiving more help from their children, still list *lack of shared responsibility in the home* as a high stress. "It isn't that the kids don't do a lot —they do—but I am just so tired and worn down by my job, kids, money, what-have-you, that I don't want to clean at 8:00 P.M.," said a single mother. Others echo her weariness. As I mentioned before, the children of the single parent recognize her dual roles and respond accordingly by taking a greater part in family responsibilities, and yet they may resent being expected to perform chores which she previously performed for them, even though they know how tired she is.

Most of these families, single- or dual-parented, pitch in and do weekly cleaning together on Saturday and let things slide the rest of the week. They are also willing to live with lowered housekeeping standards, as are all working women.

When I spoke on stress and the single-parent family at a national convention and mentioned that I was not including single caregiving fathers in my research because there were not enough in my survey group to offer valid conclusions, a single father of four protested. Canadian family counselor Ed LeClair later sent me a privately published paper on the unique stresses of families parented by single fathers. The stress I was most struck by was that fathers don't know much about housekeeping, just as suddenly-single mothers don't know much about work outside the home if they haven't been there before the divorce.

"The male single parent has all the concerns in managing a household as does the female; in most cases of course the male is placed in the position of having to learn all of the homemaking skills previously the responsibility of the female, and must manage somehow to accommodate it with a full-time job," writes LeClair. Perhaps as we see more shared custody and more men as primary caregivers, we will see the emergence of classes in homemaking skills for the single-parent father as we have seen those in work skills for the displaced homemaker.

3. Stress-reduced families lower their housekeeping standards.

Housekeeping standards appeared as a stress on women's lists but not on men's. This begs the question: are the standards self-imposed or does the stress stem from husbands' and society's expectations? Probably both. But two things are very clear: the first area of life that suffers when a woman goes to work is the couple's social life, particularly that of entertaining at home, and the second area is the quality of housekeeping. Nothing is quite as clean as it used to be in stress-effective families. A friend of mine who went to work after years of being an immaculate housekeeper said, "I used to demand a squeaky clean floor. Now, if we don't stick to it or hear it when we walk on it, I don't clean it." An exaggeration maybe but close to the truth in many families, I found.

I found many husbands who prefer lowered housekeeping standards. They mentioned that it doesn't bother them to eat more prepared foods, wear dryer-ironed shirts, and live with more clutter. "She used to drive us nuts with her cleaning," said one. "Now we are all more relaxed in a messier home."

In her book *Family Politics*, Letty Cottin Pogrebin writes, "My husband can never understand why so many men insist that their wives stay home and serve them and thus become the kind of dull, harassed drudges that the men never would have married in the first place. After transforming his bright young bride into a matronly household servant, the guy leaves her because he says he's 'outgrown' her. Yet it never occurs to him to share the drudgery and thus also share the growth when drudgery is done."[8]

Finally, in a dramatic vein, some women are going on strike to get more help in household care. One enterprising woman named Mary Ellen has developed MEE Enterprises. For $6.95, you can buy a kit that includes a "Mom on Strike" pin, a bumper sticker that reads "Give Mom a Break," and a poster that lists the grievances and lets the family know that you are on strike. A booklet which comes with the kit gives the warning signals of a mom about to strike, how to strike, and how to settle the strike. Finally, there is a sample contract for the family to read, negotiate, and sign.[9] This action may be a bit drastic for some families, but it does call attention to the widespread dissatisfaction some women feel and the stress it causes in their family life.

4. Healthy families are sympathetic with poor working situations.

Unhappiness with work situation appeared as a high stress for married men and single mothers. When people are unhappy at work, they tend to become morose, angry, despondent, and cynical, particularly if they feel locked into their jobs and helpless to change. They don't turn off these negative feelings when they leave work; instead, they bring them home. Studies have found a clear relationship, for example, between one's lack of work satisfaction and the tendency toward alcoholism and family abuse.

Thousands of adults are in jobs they hate and from which they see no escape. Some of their families are among the most stressful, but in others, these unhappy workers find comfort and support that offset the eight hours of daily misery. What creates the difference?

Families who empathize with a parent in an unpleasant job and who show gratitude for his or her perseverance because of their needs are clearly the most stress-reduced. Although the worker may be unhappy for eight hours a day, if he or she has a caring, supportive family, the work stress is minimized. "I don't like my job, no," one husband said. "But I don't mind it as long as I can think of coming home to my kids and wife."

If, however, an unhappy worker comes home to an unbonded, demanding, and strained family, stress is maximized, and no relief valve exists to reduce it. So one feature of the stress-effective family is its supportive and sympathetic stance regarding work. "I know John dislikes his work," one woman said, "but in these times, it's all there is, so we try to make life as pleasant as possible for him at home and to do something he likes on weekends so he'll have something to look forward to."

In the Traditional Value System, many men were forced into jobs they disliked for a lifetime. They accepted such roles, just as women accepted housework drudgery. This is changing today as some families encourage a change of jobs or a move, even though it means less money. "We could have retired at forty from the military with a fair pension," one wife told me. "But the wear and tear on my husband and the family wasn't worth it. We weren't willing to sacrifice the good years when our children were growing up by living with his tension and unhappiness. We're struggling financially now but we're much happier." Decisions like this were unlikely in the Traditional Value System, but are now becoming more common.

Likewise, single parents are often forced to take unpleasant jobs because of their survival needs. It is little wonder that they are the most stressed of all. If they have overwhelming money worries, responsibility for the children, household duties, *and* unpleasant work without the support of a partner, they can feel utterly overwhelmed. "I would like to get sick," a single mother told me wistfully, "but it would just increase my problems."

Children are the chief supports of single mothers who are unhappy in their work situations. In spite of family counselors' cautions, those who most help alleviate the stress are those most willing to listen to her complain about work-related problems. She has nobody else to whom she can vent about work, but at the same time she is the sole ventee for her children's worries and complaints. "I don't want to burden my kids with my job miseries but I have to talk to someone," a single parent told me. It was a familiar comment, one I heard many times from single parents.

5. Stress-effective families minimize guilt.

It follows that *guilt for not accomplishing more* would be chosen as a high stress for women because they are attempting to combine more roles than in the past. And they tend to focus on what they do not accomplish rather than upon their accomplishments. "Every time I visit my mother who is fifty-five, she takes me down to the basement and shows me her jars of canned goods and then to her sewing room to show me the quilts she's making and I feel so guilty," said a mother of four who also holds a part-time job. "I can't even get my ironing done."

Guilt stems from a variety of sources: a cultural attitude that conveys the idea that a woman should be able to do everything, or that a woman shouldn't work or use prepared foods; doubts over whether the child care is adequate and good for the child; worries about the lack of time available to husband and children; inability to keep high housekeeping standards; desire for personal fulfillment. One fact stands out from my research—*women feel guiltier than men.* Even when both work, men do not carry the same guilt their wives do over child care, for example. He may worry about the cost, but she worries about long-term effects, wondering if her working will cause the child problems down the road.

Dianne Hales says, " 'The guilt' seems to lie just below the surface of women's lives. It weasels its way into our conversation . . . we can't let go of the shape of our never-firm-enough thighs or the state of our never-clean-enough houses. It nags, like a small insistent voice whining within us, reminding us of all the promises we never kept and all the expectations we never met."

She adds, "Freud speculated that women may be naturally prone to self-condemnation. Psychiatrists since have traced the origins of women's guilt to cultural rather than biological sources, to what one analyst called the 'tyranny of the should.'

Traditionally, women learned that they 'should' be nurturers, selfless givers of life and love. The '80s challenge us with a whole new set of shoulds—as supermothers, sensuous lovers, feminine feminists, working wonder women."[10]

Dr. Theresa Larsen Crenshaw talks about the woman who feels guilty about what she "should" be able to accomplish but can't. "She works at a paying job from 8:00 A.M. to 5:00 P.M. In her 'spare' time she fixes meals, gets the children off to school, shops, cleans, cooks, chauffeurs, cheers at Little League games, always looks good and is available for sex whenever her husband wants her. She tries to be the Perfect Wife.

"When the world isn't looking, she complains bitterly, is chronically tired, depressed, resentful and occasionally suicidal. She feels so guilty that she can't take even a few minutes to relax without feeling she ought to be doing something else—like scrubbing the floor. She is in a vicious cycle that sabotages her self-esteem and puts sex on a back-burner —sometimes indefinitely."[11]

From working with women in stress seminars, I noticed a cycle which operates among women who move from high stress to controlled stress in their lives:

- Stage One: "I can be and do everything for everyone in my life." (This stage abounds with built-in failure and ongoing guilt.)
- Stage Two: "I can't be and do everything for everyone in my life." (In this stage a woman begins to accept herself.)
- Stage Three: "I don't want to be and do everything." (Freedom to choose and prioritize are the rewards of this stage.)

There may be a fourth stage which can be either positive or negative: "I won't be or do anything." Although this can be an honest action statement by a woman who has become her own person, it can also be a cop-out or a retaliatory device by a woman too tired or too angry to care about others any longer.

I ask women to estimate the age at which each stage occurs. At what age do they first embrace Stage One, and at what age do they move out of it to Stage Two, if they do? Generally, I have found that Stage One—"I can be and do everything for everyone in my life"—coincides with marriage and early parenting (the Gung Ho stage referred to in *Parent Burnout*), and that Stage Two begins as their children progress through elementary school. Sadly, some women never leave Stage One and remain chronic failures in their own eyes, chronically guilty, and chronically disenchanted with their lives. They're trying as hard as they can, and they fail, fail, fail.

Stress-effective mothers and their families accept the way things are and use their energy on solutions rather than on feeling guilty. Countless women told of leaving guilt behind, of passing through the stages just described. "I used to feel guilty if my home wasn't spotless and if I didn't cook from scratch every night but I don't feel that way any more," said one. "I accept my limitations and I prioritize. If my family can't live with it, it's their problem, not mine."

Sounds callous in the Traditional Value System but not in the Emerging one, wherein spouses tend to help minimize the guilt both verbally and emotionally. "Don't worry about the house" is a common reassurance from a spouse, or "Let's eat take-out chicken tonight."

In the *Parents With Careers Workbook*, authors Michele M. Basen and Rebecca S. Ashery point out that guilt comes from the myth that today's woman can do everything. She can't, they hold, and the response is to cut corners. "The reality is that it is tough to divide yourself between work and family. It is tough to juggle, and there are plenty who drop out for awhile."

They advise women to keep in mind that time is their most precious commodity and there are ways to make the most of it. "Need to buy something special for your cousin's wedding? Don't pound the pavement and look in every shop. Use the Yellow Pages." Or, "Your child has to go to the allergist once a week for shots. Don't beg your boss for extra leave. Pay someone to take him. And don't feel guilty."

They clearly believe that parents can be caring and responsible and still cut corners. "You must set priorities regarding your level of career commitment according to what is important at each stage of your life," they write. "Trade-offs are unavoidable. Even super women must make trade-offs some-where along the line."[12]

A great deal of guilt arises over the question of children and the effect of two parents working, but stress-effective families tend to focus on the pluses rather than the drawbacks, on reality rather than fears. One publisher told me that his wife was asked to fill in at an office temporarily. "My wife and I were terribly stressed when she went to work for three months," he said, "but the kids liked it. They (seven-year-old twins) got along beautifully; rode the bus, went to Grandma's, and were a lot more responsible than when my wife was at home. I think they were disappointed when she quit work."

While some of the children I interviewed would have pre-ferred having their mothers home full-time, more reported they prefer life with her working outside the home. I noted with interest that the girls I interviewed were much more supportive of their mothers' working than were the boys. This difference may also be attributed to the movement from the Traditional Value System to the Emerging Value System. Just as husbands resent being asked to assume more responsi-bilities in the home and to support a wife in her work, so too can sons.

The at-home mother experiences guilt of a different kind. She feels guilty because she *isn't* working. Many of these mothers surfaced in my interviews. They don't have to work and they don't want to work, but they feel that society is telling them they *should* work. "It was okay as long as the children were preschoolers," said one. "But the day my last one went into first grade, people started asking me, 'Now, what are you going to do?' as if everything I had been doing disappeared. Did they honestly think that all I did all day was entertain my child?"

Stress-reduced families with mothers at home grant her a great deal of support and affirmation. Many of these, in fact, are the least stressed of all the families interviewed because she is happy being home and they are happy having her at home. Verbally and emotionally they express this in many ways. But the chief support comes from her husband, who does not take her services for granted. "Nancy makes my life," a husband emphasized. "She's a joy to come home to and I am exceedingly grateful she doesn't feel a need to work."

In questioning these women, I found out why. Their husbands genuinely and constantly acknowledge and value their wives' work and activities. These women enjoy a number of volunteer and sports activities which would be impossible if they held outside jobs. They love entertaining, and their husbands admire their ability to host gatherings. These women get more strokes as stay-at-home mothers than many women who combine home and jobs get from their spouses and employers together.

6. Healthy families have feelings of self-worth and esteem.

Guilt leads us into the stress of low self-esteem, low self-worth, and feelings of unattractiveness, which appeared on the lists of both married women and single mothers but which appeared hardly at all on the men's list. In fact, I found an astounding difference in percentages, the greatest variance between men and women in any of the stresses: *52 percent of single mothers chose low self-esteem as a high stress, as did 34 percent of married women. But only 1 percent of the men named it as a stress.*

Low self-esteem, then, would seem to be a woman's stress. However, when I discussed this with various groups in stress workshops, men objected to this conclusion, emphasizing that culturally men are not permitted to admit to low self-esteem, so they automatically dismiss it as a choice. Many men in the groups acknowledged low self-esteem, adding, "But I would never admit it on a survey because it isn't manly . . . you aren't on top of things. The game is to pretend you're in control at all times."

So we don't know if this low figure represents men's real or artificial self-esteem. We do know that self-esteem is closely linked with power, particularly earning power in our country, with attractiveness, and with the amount of control we have over our lives and what is happening to us. When we have sufficient control to be able to express our opinions, to make decisions regarding our daily lives, and to plan for our future, our self-esteem is heightened.

Self-esteem is basically a sense of worthiness. Am I worth anything as a person? A paper on the subject says, "Persons with high self-esteem appear poised and confident. Their social relationships are generally good. They are less influenced by peers and tend to make better decisions. People with low self-esteem, on the other hand, may feel isolated, unloved, and defenseless. They perceive themselves as being powerless to attain what they desire from life. Often, withdrawal and passivity are the results."[3]

It follows that people with high self-esteem feel more in control, and this gives them even higher self-esteem while the reverse is true in those with low self-esteem. When a woman does not feel good about herself, she is less able to relate openly and more likely to be defensive, anxious, and critical. This extends to the family and intensifies stress.

Women worry more than men about personal attractiveness. And it can become a great strain in a marriage if it is a high value to their spouse. "Jim tells me he doesn't mind my being forty as long as I don't look forty," a wife reported. "He looks forty but that's okay. It just isn't fair. I'm going to look forty sometime and what then?" Beneath her words lies a fear that haunts many women: will he love (leave?) me if I age?

Television, movies, and our cosmetic culture feed into this fear, which suggests that perhaps a low self-image among women is not personally imposed as much as culturally imposed. Elissa Melamed, author of *Mirror Mirror: The Terror of Not Being Young,* points out, "Some of us have the luxury of the kind of time and money it takes to keep looking youthful but a lot of women don't. And as a group we don't have the right to age in an ordinary way. We all should have a right to age any way we please—just as men do. Why should we starve ourselves, go under the plastic surgeon's knife, for God's sake? Men don't feel they're not OK as they get a little beer belly, begin to bald or go gray."[4]

Her comment led me to recall the time I was on a plane and two men behind me made numerous uncomplimentary jokes about a flight attendant in her late forties. She was attentive and attractive, but she was gray-haired. They commented that the airline must have scraped the bottom of the barrel and how they missed the attractive young stewardesses of yore. When we landed and I turned around to look at them, I was astonished to see that they were both in their fifties, one gray and one bald. I doubt if the irony of their words even occurred to them.

The members of stress-effective families I studied have good self-esteem. They feel good about themselves, even though they by no means all fit the media image of attractiveness. Their spouses and children let them know that they are attractive and worthwhile.

7. Stress-effective families are optimistic and bonded in a caring relationship.

These families undergo the same struggles in changing role patterns and value systems as highly stressed families, but they develop skills to meet conflicts and resentments *as they arise*. They don't put them off thinking they may go away but address them as soon as they perceive them. They make use of communication and conflict-resolution skills discussed earlier. Most importantly, they collaborate constantly on issues that show signs of straining family life, including feelings of failure and guilt.

I am impressed at these families' ability to adapt and to seek support from each other and those outside the immediate family. Their family life is not set in stone but is flexible. When there's a change of jobs, hormones, or behavior, they talk about it, share feelings, and come up with ways of smoothing the transition. These families clearly demonstrate a caring bondedness. They work as a unit; stress is perceived as *our* problem, not just *your* problem.

And they care about one another. If one person is unhappy about his job or her housework, everyone shares a bit of that unhappiness. It becomes a family issue, and everyone takes responsibility for helping to resolve it. It is a joy to observe these families, many of whom have experienced and overcome multiple stresses. Their very bearing conveys what they might say: "We know we can handle this because we have handled worse in the past, and we know we have each other for support." Where the family relationship is strong, caring, and communicative, family stress is minimized. Time, work, children, and money pressures exist, but in stress-reduced families, they are viewed as normal and manageable.

In summary, stress-effective families
1. are embracing a new value system,
2. share responsibilities around the home,
3. live with lowered housekeeping standards,
4. empathize with spouse or parents unhappy in their jobs,
5. minimize guilt,
6. have good self-esteem,
7. exhibit a family bonding and optimism that tells them they can handle any ordinary stress.

Some Reflective Conclusions on Family Stress

After researching, interviewing, and living with family stress the past two years, I find myself being asked, "What did you learn? Is family stress here to stay? Are you hopeful or fearful about the future of the family and its ability to manage in a stressful society?"

What did I learn? Here are twelve conclusions that deserve reflection by families as well as institutions and workplaces interested in alleviating stress in families.

CONCLUSIONS ON FAMILY STRESS

1. Husbands and wives vary significantly on what they perceive as top stresses within the same family.
2. Work stresses are allowed to impact the family, but family stresses are not allowed to impact work.
3. Four of the ten most-named stressors in family life have to do with lack of time.
4. Healthy families view stresses as normal, while other families view them as evidence of weakness or failure.
5. Healthy families seek solutions, while stressful families seek blame.
6. Resolving one family stress often gives rise to another equally stressful.
7. The named stress is not always the actual stress.
8. While insufficient money is named as the top stress in most families, the real stress stems from how money is viewed and spent rather than the amount available.
9. Low self-image/self-worth is overwhelmingly a woman's stress.

10. Enjoyable volunteer activity reduces a person's stress level while unenjoyable volunteer activity increases it.

11. The ability to deal effectively with stress is related to how much prior experience the family has had in coping with stress: the more stress experienced, the more skills developed.

12. Stress-effective families distinguish between stresses they can and cannot control. They focus their energy on controllable stresses and live with the others.

As sobering as these conclusions may be, I am more hopeful than fearful about the family's ability to deal with everyday stress because, as a culture, we are finally recognizing and addressing stresses as they emerge. The workplace is beginning to acknowledge responsibility in helping families manage work-related stresses. Government, schools, churches, and communities are doing likewise.

Families themselves are becoming more vocal and more insistent that the pressures they inherit from society be addressed, not by themselves alone but by the whole of society. But most encouraging, I found multiple skills being developed within stress-effective families which are beginning to be shared and imitated by other families.

The "stress for success" value system is breaking down. Healthy families are turning instead to "relate for success" and "relax for success." The work ethic is being questioned and found wanting, increasingly replaced with a life ethic that says there's more to life than work and monetary success.

All of this is exciting and hopeful. I interviewed families who have made dramatic turnarounds in eliminating pressures and increasing pleasures in modern family life. Their stories needed sharing, and I hope I was able to do so in this book.

As eighty-two-year-old Marguerite, who's lived through most of this century's wars, depressions, and changes, said it, "Lordy, what is all this talk of stress these days? Stress is life, that's all. It's God's way of showing us we're alive and kicking. We just got to kick a little harder some times, right?"

Right. And that's what healthy families are doing.

Notes

CHAPTER 1

1. Patti Thorn, "Family Fights to Break Grip of Rare Disease," *Rocky Mountain News,* March 27, 1984.
2. "Stress: Can We Cope?" *Time,* June 6, 1983.
3. David H. Olson, Hamilton I. McCubbin, et al, *Families: What Makes Them Work* (Beverly Hills: Sage Publications, 1983).
4. George Monaghan, "Now She Knows of Stress Firsthand," *Minneapolis Tribune,* March 11, 1984.

CHAPTER 2

1. Glenn Collins, "'Normal' Children Studied for Stress," *New York Times,* October 16, 1983.

CHAPTER 3

1. Ronald M. Sabatelli, "The Marital Comparison Level Index: A Social Exchange Measure of Marital Satisfaction," unpublished paper.
2. Carol Tavris, "The Myth of the 50/50 Marriage," *Woman's Day,* March 6, 1984.
3. "Around the Network," *Family Therapy NetWorker,* March-April 1984.
4. Michael Griffin, O.C.D., "The Stresses of Intimacy," *Spiritual Life,* 1979.
5. Diane Hales, "Marriages That Get Better and Better," *McCall's,* January 1983.
6. Rick Selvin, "Author Claims Women Can Change Their Men," *Denver Post,* January 8, 1984.
7. Carin Rubinstein and Phillip Shaver, *In Search of Intimacy* (New York: Delacorte Press, 1982).

8. Sharon Dreyer, *Care of the Mentally Ill* (Santa Cruz, Calif.: Davis Publishing Co., 1977).
9. Steven Naifeh and Gregory White Smith, *Why Can't Men Open Up?: Overcoming Men's Fear of Intimacy* (New York: Clarkson N. Potter, 1984).
10. Philip Blumstein and Pepper Schwartz, "What Makes Today's Marriages Last?" *Family Weekly*, November 13, 1983.
11. Robert E. Emery, "Interpersonal Conflict and the Children of Discord and Divorce," *Psychological Bulletin* (92) 2.
12. Marty Meitus, "Therapist Supports Shared Parenting," *Rocky Mountain News*, February 12, 1984.
13. Kristine Miller Tomasik, "When Couples Disagree," *Catholic Digest*, December 1983.
14. Ibid.
15. Naifeh and Smith, op. cit.
16. Tomasik, op. cit.
17. Ibid.
18. Ibid.
19. Hamilton I. McCubbin and Charles R. Figley, eds., *Stress and the Family: Coping with Normative Transitions*, vol. 1 (New York: Brunner/Mazel, 1983).
20. Ibid.
21. Barbara Holland, "Babies Aren't as Cheap as Yachts But They're a Lot More Fun," *McCall's*, June 1983.
22. Sue Miller, "Marital Woes Result from Post-childbirth," *Baltimore Evening Sun*, November 8, 1983.
23. Maxine Hancock, *People in Process* (Old Tappan, N.J.: Fleming H. Revell, 1978).
24. McCubbin and Figley, op. cit.

CHAPTER 4

1. Philip Blumstein and Pepper Schwartz, *American Couples: Money, Work, Sex* (New York: William Morrow, 1983).
2. Nat B. Read, "In Debt Do We Part," *Denver Post*, November 6, 1983.
3. Aileen Jacobsen, "In Matters of the Heart," *Denver Post*, October 23, 1983.
4. Blumstein and Schwartz, op. cit.
5. Ibid.
6. David Mace, "Marriage Matters," *Marriage and Family Living*, January 1984.

7. The General Mills American Family Report, 1978-79, *Family Health in an Era of Stress* (Minneapolis: General Mills, 1979).

8. John W. Wright, *American Almanac of Jobs and Salaries* (New York: Avon, 1984).

9. Paul C. Rosenblatt and Linda Olson Keller, "Economic Vulnerability and Economic Stress in Farm Couples," *Family Relations,* October 1983.

10. "The Average American Family, Then and Now," *U.S. News & World Report,* November 21, 1983.

11. Holland, op. cit.

12. McCubbin, op. cit.

13. Aileen Jacobsen, op. cit.

14. Jane Anderson, "Earning Isn't Only Money Skill Children Need," *Christian Science Monitor,* November 14, 1983.

15. Joseph L. Felix, "Parenting Tips," *Marriage and Family Living,* November 1983.

16. Grace W. Weinstein, "What Nobody Else Will Tell Your Child About Money," *McCall's,* March 1984.

17. Felix, op. cit.

18. Jane Anderson, op. cit.

19. Ruth Walker, "Work Can Spell Trouble for Some Teen Students," *Christian Science Monitor,* February 15, 1984.

CHAPTER 5

1. Catherine S. Chilman, "Significant Differences Between Parents with High Satisfaction Scores and Those with Low Scores: 1973 and 1981." Unpublished abstract, University of Wisconsin, Milwaukee.

2. Germaine Greer, *Sex and Destiny* (New York: Harper & Row, 1984).

3. Ibid.

4. Sharon Epstein, "Counseling Helps," *Marriage and Family Living,* June 1984.

5. Joan Herst, "Kids Sense Vulnerability," *Denver Post,* September 25, 1983.

6. Foster W. Cline, Ph.D., public lecture, Littleton, Colorado, 1984.

7. Eleanor Berman, *The Cooperating Family* (Englewood Cliffs, N.J.: Prentice-Hall, 1977).

8. Foster W. Cline, op. cit.

9. Margaret Jaworski, "Are We Making Our Children Grow Up Too Fast?" *Family Circle,* March 16, 1982.

10. Susan Schiffer Stautberg, "The Rat Race Isn't for Tots," *New York Times,* August 7, 1984.

11. Joseph Procaccini, "The New Energy Crisis: Parent Burnout," *Marriage and Family Living,* October 1983.

12. Sandy Battin, "The Loss of Innocence," *Denver Post,* August 7, 1983.

13. Herbert Hendin, *The Age of Sensation* (New York: Norton, 1977).

14. Ross D. Parke, *Fathers* (Cambridge: Harvard University Press, 1981).

15. Jim Brieg, "This One's For You, Dad," *U.S. Catholic,* June 1984.

16. Joseph Procaccini, op. cit.

17. Dr. Lee Salk, "Preparing Children for the Grownup World," *McCall's,* September 1983.

18. Urie Bronfenbrenner, "An Ecological Perspective," *The American Family: Current Perspectives,* Harvard Seminar Series (Cambridge: Harvard University Press, 1979).

19. John A. Jenkins, "For the Kids' Sake," *The Ambassador,* March 1983.

20. Lynne Ames, "For Children of the Divorced, a Course on How to Cope," *New York Times,* December 12, 1984.

21. Verna Noel Jones, "Most Underachievers Can Change," *Rocky Mountain News,* February 29, 1984.

22. Judy Mann, "What to Do with a Violent, Sneaky Child," *Denver Post,* November 6, 1983.

23. Foster W. Cline, op. cit.

24. Dr. Lee Salk, "Trying to Be Fair with Your Children," *McCall's,* November 1983.

25. Susan Sherman Fadem, "When Men Won't Grow Up," *Denver Post,* October 16, 1983.

26. Thomas Lickona, *Raising Good Children* (New York: Bantam, 1983).

27. George Durrant, "How to Talk to Your Teenager," The Church of Jesus Christ of Latter-Day Saints publication.

28. Thomas Lickona, op. cit.

29. Don Wegscheider, *If Only My Family Understood Me* (Minneapolis: CompCare, 1983).

30. Dolores Curran, *Traits of a Healthy Family* (Minneapolis: Winston Press, 1983).

31. Carole and Andrew Calladine, *Raising Brothers and Sisters Without Raising the Roof* (Minneapolis: Winston Press, 1979).
32. Foster W. Cline, op. cit.
33. Betsy Hoke, "Parent as Cheerleader," workshop at Metropolitan State College, Denver, Colorado, 1984.
34. Foster W. Cline, op. cit.
35. Kate Perry, "Study Offers View of What Makes Families Strong," *Minneapolis Star-Tribune,* December 2, 1983.
36. McCubbin and Figley, op. cit.
37. Myron Brenton, *How to Survive Your Child's Rebellious Teens* (New York: J. B. Lippincott, 1979).
38. Carl Pickhardt, "Parenting Tips," *Marriage and Family Living,* December 1983.
39. *Bringing Religion Home Newsletter,* February 1984.
40. Carl Pickhardt, "Parenting Tips," *Marriage and Family Living,* January 1984.
41. Christopher Connell, "Insurance Study Finds Baby Boom Generation Independent, Traditional," *San Antonio Light,* December 7, 1983.
42. Carl Pickhardt, op. cit.
43. Philip B. Taft, Jr., "Parents VS. Peers," *Family Circle,* November 1983.

CHAPTER 6

1. *The New Relationships Newsletter,* November-December 1983.
2. Stephen A. Timm, "Making the Family Work," *Northwest Orient,* February 1984.
3. Bob Greene, "The Twitching of America Is Everywhere," *Rocky Mountain News,* July 25, 1983.
4. Ibid.
5. Dolores Curran, op. cit.
6. Barrie S. Greiff, "The Executive Family," *The American Family: Current Perspectives,* Harvard Seminar Series (Cambridge: Harvard University Press, 1979).
7. Timm, op. cit.
8. Blumstein and Schwartz, op. cit.
9. *New Relationships,* op. cit.
10. Blumstein and Schwartz, op. cit.
11. Diane Hales, "He Comes Home But He Really Isn't Here," *McCall's,* March 1984.

12. Wayne Rickerson, *We Never Have Time Just for Us* (Ventura, Calif.: Regal Books, 1982).
13. "Neighbors," *Woman's Day,* February 7, 1984.
14. "Neighbors," *Woman's Day,* May 22, 1984.
15. Martin G. Olsen, "Double Income, Double Trouble?" *Marriage and Family Living,* December 1983.
16. *Time,* op. cit.
17. Curran, op. cit.
18. Blumstein and Schwartz, op. cit.
19. Olsen, op. cit.
20. Ronna Romney and Beppie Harrison, "Friendship and Sharing Play Vital Roles in Successful Marriage," *Denver Post,* December 5, 1983.
21. Wayne E. Oates, "Finding Time for Your Spouse," *Marriage and Family Living,* November 1982.
22. Blumstein and Schwartz, op. cit.
23. Donald A. Tubesing, *Kicking Your Stress Habits* (Duluth, Minn.: Whole Person Press, 1981).
24. Ibid.
25. Blumstein and Schwartz, op. cit.
26. Susan Jacoby, "I'm Lonely," *McCall's,* September 1983.
27. Tubesing, op. cit.
28. Timm, op. cit.
29. Tubesing, op. cit.

CHAPTER 7

1. Blumstein and Schwartz, op. cit.
2. Zick Rubin, "Are Working Wives Hazardous to Their Husband's Mental Health?" *Psychology Today,* May 1983.
3. Blumstein and Schwartz, op. cit.
4. Ibid.
5. Ibid.
6. Ibid.
7. Hendin, op. cit.
8. Letty Cottin Pogrebin, *Family Politics* (New York: McGraw-Hill, 1983).
9. MEE Enterprises, P.O. Box 441, San Ramon, Calif. 94583.
10. Diane Hales, "You've Done Your Best. Why Do You Still Feel Guilty?" *McCall's,* June 1983.
11. Theresa Larsen Crenshaw, "Too Tired to Care? How to Enjoy Sex Again," *Woman's Day,* June 7, 1983.

12. Nancy Minkoff, "Juggling Family and Career," *Denver Post*, November 13, 1983.
13. Mary Nelson, "Our Children's Self-Esteem" (Santa Cruz, Calif.: Network Publications, 1983).
14. Sue Mullin, "Elissa Melamed: Aging with Pride," *Washington Times*, March 1984.

Sources

Aldous, J., ed. *Two Paychecks: Life in Dual-Earner Families.* Beverly Hills: Sage Publications, 1982.

The American Family: Current Perspectives. Six tapes from the Harvard Seminar Series. Cambridge: Harvard University Press, 1981.

Badinter, E. *Mother Love: Myth and Reality.* New York: Macmillan, 1981.

Berman, E. *The Cooperating Family.* Englewood Cliffs, N.J.: Prentice-Hall, 1977.

Blumstein, P., and P. Schwartz. *American Couples: Money, Work, Sex.* New York: William Morrow, 1983.

Boss, P. et al. *The Father's Role in Family Systems: An Annotated Bibliography.* Madison: University of Wisconsin Press, 1979.

Brazelton, T. B. *On Becoming a Family.* New York: Macmillan, 1983.

Brenton, M. *How to Survive Your Child's Rebellious Teens.* New York: J. B. Lippincott, 1979.

Calladine, C., and A. Calladine. *Raising Brothers and Sisters Without Raising the Roof.* Minneapolis: Winston Press, 1979.

Committee on Child Development Research and Public Policy. *American Families and the Economy: The High Costs of Living.* Washington, D.C.: National Academy Press, 1983.

Clarke, J. I. *Self-Esteem: A Family Affair.* Minneapolis: Winston Press, 1982.

Cretcher, D. *Steering Clear: Helping Your Child Through the High-Risk Drug Years.* Minneapolis: Winston Press, 1982.

Curran, D. *Traits of a Healthy Family.* Minneapolis: Winston Press, 1983.

Davitz, L. L. *Baby Hunger: Every Woman's Longing for a Baby.* Minneapolis: Winston Press, 1984.

Drane, J. *Your Emotional Life and What You Can Do About It.* Chicago: Thomas More Press, 1984.

Dreikurs, R. *Challenges of Parenthood.* New York: Dutton, 1979.

Dreikurs, R., and V. Soltz. *Children: the Challenge.* New York: Dutton, 1964.

Eastman, M. *Education for Family Life: A Survey of Available Programs and Their Evaluation.* Melbourne: Institute of Family Studies, 1983.

Elkind, D. *The Hurried Child.* Reading, Mass.: Addison-Wesley, 1981.

Employed Parents and Their Children: A Data Book. Washington, D.C.: Children's Defense Fund, 1983.

Erikson, E. *Identity, Youth and Crisis.* New York: Norton, 1968.

Faber, A., and E. Mazlish. *How to Talk So Kids Will Listen & Listen So Kids Will Talk.* New York: Avon Books, 1982.

Finley, M. K. *Christian Families in the Real World.* Chicago: Thomas More Press, 1984.

Fontenelle, D. H. *Understanding and Managing Overactive Children.* Englewood Cliffs, N.J.: Prentice-Hall, 1983.

Gallup, G., Jr. *Emerging Trends.* Princeton: Princeton Religion Research Center, 1984.

Gesell, A., F. Ilg, and L. Ames. *The Child from Five to Ten.* New York: Harper & Row, 1977.

Goodloe, A., J. Bensahel, and J. Kelly. *Managing Yourself: How to Control Emotion, Stress, and Time.* New York: Franklin Watts, 1984.

Goodman, E. *Turning Points.* New York: Doubleday, 1979.

Greer, G. *Sex and Destiny.* New York: Harper & Row, 1984.

Greiff, B. S. and P. Munter. *Tradeoffs: Executive, Family and Organizational Life.* New York: New American Library, 1980.

Hancock, M. *People in Process.* Old Tappan, N.J.: Fleming H. Revell, 1978.

Harris, L. et al. *Families at Work: Strengths and Strains.* Minneapolis: General Mills, 1981.

Hayes, C. D. and S. B. Kamerman, eds. *Children of Working Parents: Experiences and Outcomes.* Washington, D.C.: National Academy Press, 1983.

Heffner, E. *Mothering: How Women Can Enjoy a New Productive Relationship with Their Children—and a New Image of Themselves.* New York: Doubleday, 1980.

Hendin, H. *The Age of Sensation.* New York: Norton, 1977.

House, J. S. *Work, Stress, and Social Support.* Reading, Mass.: Addison-Wesley, 1981.

Jenson, G., G. Wise, and F. Aolonio. *Getting Down the Road.* Santa Cruz, Calif.: Network Publications, 1983.

Kennedy, E. *Loneliness and Everyday Problems.* New York: Doubleday, 1983.

Kimball, G. *The 50-50 Marriage.* Boston: Beacon Press, 1983.

Kinzer, N. S. *Stress and the American Woman.* New York: Ballantine, 1979.

Kolbenschlag, M. *Kiss Sleeping Beauty Good-bye.* New York: Doubleday, 1979.

Krumboltz, J., and H. Krumboltz. *Changing Children's Behavior.* Englewood Cliffs, N.J.: Prentice-Hall, 1972.

Kvols-Riedler, B., and K. Kvols-Riedler. *Redirecting Children's Misbehavior: A Guide for Cooperation Between Children and Adults.* Boulder, Colo.: R.D.I.C. Publications, 1979.

Lakein, A. *How to Get Control of Your Time and Your Life.* New York: New American Library, 1973.

Lamm, D. *Second Banana.* Boulder, Colo.: Johnson Books, 1983.

Lansky, Vicki. *Practical Parenting Tips for the School-Age Years.* New York: Bantam, 1985.

Lash, C. *Haven in a Heartless World: The Family Besieged.* New York: Basic Books, 1977.

Lerman, S. *Parent Awareness: Positive Parenting for the 1980s.* Minneapolis: Winston Press, 1983.

——————. *Responsive Parenting.* Circle Pines, Minn.: American Guidance Service, 1983.

Levinson, D. J. *The Seasons of a Man's Life.* New York: Ballantine, 1978.

Levitan, S. *What's Happening to the American Family?* Baltimore: Johns Hopkins University Press, 1981.

Lewis, J. M. *How's Your Family?* New York: Brunner/Mazel, 1979.

Lewis, R., ed. *Men in Difficult Times: Masculinity Today and Tomorrow.* Englewood Cliffs, N.J.: Prentice-Hall, 1981.

Lickona, T. *Raising Good Children.* New York: Bantam, 1983.

Linder, S. B. *The Harried Leisure Class.* New York: Columbia University Press, 1970.

Mace, D. and V. Mace. *How to Have a Happy Marriage.* Nashville: Abingdon Press, 1983.

Margolis, D. R. *The Managers: Corporate Life in America.* New York: William Morrow, 1979.

Masnick, G. and M. J. Bane. *The Nation's Families: 1960-1990.* Cambridge: Harvard University Press, 1980.

May, R. *The Courage to Create.* New York: Bantam, 1975.

McCubbin, H. I., A. E. Cauble, and J. M. Patterson, eds. *Family Stress, Coping, and Social Support.* Springfield, Ill.: C. Thomas, 1982.

McCubbin, H. I., and C. R. Figley, eds. *Stress and the Family.* New York: Brunner/Mazel, 1983.

Miller, S. et al. *Couple and Interpersonal Communication.* Minneapolis: Interpersonal Communication Programs, 1983.

Money, R. *Building Stronger Families.* Wheaton, Ill.: Victor Books, 1984.

Montagu, A. *The Dehumanization of Man.* New York: McGraw-Hill, 1984.

Moore, L., and K. Moore. *When You Both Go to Work.* Waco, Tex.: Word Books, 1984.

Naifeh, S., and G. W. Smith. *Why Can't Men Open Up? Overcoming Men's Fear of Intimacy.* New York: Clarkson N. Potter, 1984.

Nelson, M. *Our Children's Self-Esteem.* Santa Cruz, Calif.: Network Publications, 1983.

Neville, H., and M. Halaby. *No-Fault Parenting: A Practical Guide to Day-to-Day Life with Children under Six.* New York: Facts on File Publications, 1984.

Offer, D., E. Ostrov, and K. Howard. *The Adolescent: A Psychological Self-Portrait.* New York: Basic Books, 1981.

Olson, D. H., H. I. McCubbin, et al. *Families: What Makes Them Work.* Beverly Hills: Sage Publications, 1983.

Ornish, D. *Stress, Diet and Your Heart.* New York: Holt, Rinehart & Winston, 1982.

Parke, R. *Fathers.* Cambridge: Harvard University Press, 1981.

Paul, J., and M. Paul. *Do I Have to Give up Me to Be Loved by You?* Minneapolis: CompCare, 1983.

Peck, M. S. *The Road Less Traveled.* New York: Simon and Schuster, 1978.

Pileggi, S. *If You Love Your Kids ... Don't Let Them Grow up to Be Jerks.* La Jolla, Calif.: Oak Tree Publications, 1980.

Pogrebin, L. C. *Family Politics.* New York: McGraw-Hill, 1983.

Procaccini, J., and M. Kiefaber. *Parent Burnout.* New York: Doubleday, 1983.

———. *P.L.U.S. Parenting: Take Charge of Your Family.* New York: Doubleday, 1985.

Rickerson, W. *We Never Have Time Just for Us.* Ventura, Calif.: Regal Books, 1982.

Rhodes, S., and J. Wilson. *Surviving Family Life: The Seven Crises of Living Together.* New York: Putnam, 1981.

Rogers, F., and B. Head. *Mister Rogers Talks with Parents.* New York: Berkley, 1983.

Rossman, P. *Family Survival: Coping with Stress.* New York: Pilgrim Press, 1984.

Rubin, T. I., and E. Rubin. *Not to Worry: The American Family Book of Mental Health.* New York: Viking, 1984.

Rubinstein, C. and P. Shaver. *In Search of Intimacy.* New York: Delacorte Press, 1982.

Russell, G. *The Changing Role of Fathers?* St. Lucia, Australia: University of Queensland Press, 1983.

Salk, L. *The Complete Dr. Salk: A-Z Guide to Raising Your Child.* New York: New American Library, 1985.

Scanzoni, J. *Sexual Bargaining: Power Politics in the American Marriage.* New York: Prentice-Hall, 1972.

——————. *Shaping Tomorrow's Family: Theory and Policy for the 21st Century.* Beverly Hills: Sage Publications, 1983.

Schaef, A. *Women's Reality.* Minneapolis: Winston Press, 1981.

Schowalter, J. E. and W. R. Anyam. *The Family Handbook of Adolescence: A Comprehensive Medically Oriented Guide to the Years From Puberty to Adulthood.* New York: Alfred A. Knopf, 1979.

Sehnert, K. *Stress/Unstress.* Minneapolis: Augsburg, 1981.

Skolnick, A., and J. H. Skolnick. *Family in Transition.* Boston: Little, Brown, 1980.

Staines, G. L., and J. H. Pleck. *The Impact of Work Schedules on the Family.* Ann Arbor, Mich.: University of Michigan, 1983.

Stinnett, N. *Relationships in Marriage and the Family.* New York: Macmillan, 1984.

Strommen, M. P., and A. I. Strommen. *Five Cries of Parents: New Help for Families on the Issues that Trouble Them Most.* San Francisco: Harper & Row, 1985.

Sussman, M. B. *Marriage & Family Review.* New York: Haworth Press, 1984.

Timmons, T. *Stress in the Family.* Eugene, Ore.: Harvest House, 1982.

Tubesing, D. A. *Kicking Your Stress Habits.* Duluth, Minn.: Whole Person Press, 1981.

Tufte, V., and B. Myerhoff. *Changing Images of the Family.* New Haven: Yale University Press, 1979.

Voth, H. *The Castrated Family.* Kansas City: Sheed Andrews and McMeel, 1977.

Walsh, F., ed. *Normal Family Processes.* New York: Guilford Press, 1982.

Wegscheider, D. *If Only My Family Understood Me.* Minneapolis: CompCare, 1983.

Weiss, R. S. *Going It Alone: The Family, Life and Social Situation of the Single Parent.* New York: Basic Books, 1979.

Woolfork, R. L., and F. C. Richardson. *Stress, Sanity and Survival.* New York: New American Library, 1979.

Yankelovich, D. *New Rules: Searching for Fulfillment in a World Turned Upside Down.* New York: Random House, 1981.

Zimney, C. F. *In Praise of Homemaking.* Notre Dame, Ind.: Ave Maria Press, 1984.

Index

ORDER NOW!

SIX GREAT NOVELS FROM THESE BESTSELLING AUTHORS